UNIVERSITY OF
WINCHESTER

Martial Rose Library
Tel: 01962 827306

KT-147-525

KA 0157518 X

WITHDRAWN FROM
THE LIBRARY
UNIVERSITY OF
WINCHESTER

CRUELTY AND CIVILIZATION

The great spectacles of Ancient Rome were not merely casual entertainment, a matter of choice for the audience, like the modern theatre. Under the Empire, the games became a public opiate and gave the daily life of Rome its rhythm and lustre. From one year to the next, the Roman citizens lived in anticipation of the games; they provided excitement and helped the citizens forget the mediocrity of their own condition and their lack of political power.

Roland Auguet has not restricted himself to the detailed reconstruction of these spectacles, he has also analysed the emotions of the crowd and the motives of the rulers. He explains why the games were so important in the life of the city and what the popularity of these spectacles, this strange combination of *Cruelty and Civilization*, reveals about the mentality of ancient Rome.

CRUELTY AND CIVILIZATION

The Roman Games

Roland Auguet

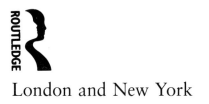

London and New York

937
AUG

0157 8X

First published in 1972 by
George Allen & Unwin Ltd

Translated from the French
Cruauté et Civilization: Les Jeux Romains
(Flammarion, Paris, 1970)

Hardback reprinted and first paperback edition published in 1994
by Routledge
11 New Fetter Lane, London EC4P 4EE

Simultaneously published in the USA and Canada
by Routledge
29 West 35th Street, New York, NY 10001

© 1972 George Allen & Unwin Ltd
© 1994 Routledge

Printed and bound in Great Britain by
Butler & Tanner Ltd, Frome and London

All rights reserved. No part of this book may be reprinted or
reproduced or utilized in any form or by any electronic,
mechanical, or other means, now known or hereafter
invented, including photocopying and recording, or in any
information storage or retrieval system, without permission in
writing from the publishers.

British Library Cataloguing in Publication Data
A catalogue record for this book is available from the British Library

Library of Congress Cataloging in Publication Data
Applied for

ISBN 0-415-10452-1   0-415-10453-X (pbk)

PREFACE

Of all the monuments left to us by the Romans the amphitheatres are the most imposing and undoubtedly the best known to the public, perhaps because some of them are still to be seen almost intact, like those at Nîmes and at Arles. Everyone knows, too, the sort of spectacles—organized shame, as historians have often stressed—which took place behind these arcades to which the Roman architects gave such a grandiose nobility.

No general study of this immense subject exists. It is a subject which involves the history of Rome and of the Roman Empire, its monumental art and its sociology; it embraces one of the most important features of the daily life of the masses and of the ruler. Naturally, within the modest limits accorded us, we have not been able to be exhaustive. We must make a choice and reject many episodes which are often relevant to the history of the games. Thus, to take one example, it is not possible to speak of the votive games without entering at great length and in the most complex detail into the political and religious problems peculiar to a given period.

We have therefore been forced to proceed by suggestive touches, with the aim of giving the reader, by a study of the spectacles, a true feeling of the city and its masses, of a civilization, and of an empire.

Finally, the abundance of the bibliography to which we have had to refer (which often means reference to articles difficult to trace) has not permitted us to give detailed references on every page. This would have forced us to overload the text of the book which, moreover, has no pretensions to erudition. We have had to content ourselves with indicating references to the most important sources in the text.

7

CONTENTS

ILLUSTRATIONS

INTRODUCTION: ROMAN CRUELTY

A special mentality?

Which of us does not recall the horrified fascination we felt as children when looking at those pictures in our school-books which came between the lowly dwellings of our ancestors the Gauls and the picturesque escarpments on which the first keeps of the Middle Ages were built? A gladiator, with movements clumsy and stiff because of his armour, half kneels and raises his hooked vizor, pierced by mysterious holes, towards an imaginary grandstand, menacing with his curved sword the man prostrate at his feet. His calm, the restraint of his gestures, his indifference, are among the things which particularly excite childish wonder. In another picture a lioness leaps upon a condemned man whose almost transparent robe still flutters on the sand; farther on, some vague figures crowd together at the approach of another wild beast; or perhaps the beast crouches, satiated, its paws doubled up over a shapeless mass, aloof and sullenly watching the dense throng of onlookers.

In one sense these pictures, a little morbid and shocking, teach us a lesson: that the life of a man has not always had the value that our own morality strives to give it. In the past it could be a mere episode, and death the instrument of a collective pleasure. But to the 'Why?' which a discovery of this sort usually suggests, the caption below the picture affords no answer. These scenes impress themselves on us because they are monstrous and inexplicable. Their apparent pointlessness incites us little by little to attribute the violence which they reveal to some cruelty in the Roman nature, a prejudice which even closer contact with the ancient world may only correct with difficulty.

There is nothing more incompatible with the Roman mentality

13

than the form of cruelty known as sadism, without which, however, it is hard to explain the continuance and success of certain of these 'games' which have retained so sinister a renown. To a great extent cruelty of this type is pointless; it destroys and consumes without advantage, to satisfy a passion or merely for pleasure. It is a luxury. But the Roman was not only a realist; he was a slave to utility in the narrowest sense. The sacrifice of what could be a source of wealth, made to satisfy a momentary instinct, a partiality or a purely subjective emotion, was for him a serious fault, a slur on the most elementary principle of his morality. That was true in small things as in large; there existed, for example, a whole series of laws aimed at prohibiting the squandering of wealth caused by burning or burying with the dead articles which had belonged to them in life. No Roman would have had his wife and his horse buried with him, like the Great Khan—there would only be small personal objects or household pets such as cats or birds. Even more forcibly, the law prohibited drenching the pyre with costly perfumes or placing gold in the coffin, with the exception, formally specified, of what the dead man might hold in his mouth.

Just as they did not tolerate the wastefulness of grief, the Romans did not surrender to the demands of vengeance. As a rule they treated the vanquished with a generosity based on calculation; they thus avoided kindling a latent desire for revenge and preserved a territory which had become for them a capital gain. Annihilation and pitiless massacre were only a last resort against an irreconcilable enemy, such as Carthage or certain Breton tribes which were exterminated *en masse* in the amphitheatre because they were too unreliable to become good soldiers and too savage to serve as slaves. They could only be treated as enemies. So realism and prudence necessitated recourse to the most violent extremes. At other times punishment was inflicted to discourage revolt and disloyalty. In this, the Romans still obeyed the dictates of calculation and not a bloodthirsty instinct. The sometimes excessive (though never arbitrary) harshness which they showed towards their own people as well as to their enemies is not to be confused with cruelty. The general who threw deserters to the beasts was no more a despot than one who razed a city to the ground. He stressed the enormity of the crime by the choice of an exceptional punishment, commensurate with the degree of shame which reflected upon the guilty.

Doubtless these sentiments could change, or at least vary, with the passage of time. But this brief analysis shows clearly that no link necessarily existed between the Roman mind and the cruelty implicit in certain games dear to the public taste, and indeed that there was, to some extent, a contradiction between the two. It would therefore be foolish to attribute their evolution and their success to a special 'mentality'; the spectacles which have aroused the censure of posterity were a product, to some extent paradoxical, of history, and the Roman taste for blood, if it ever existed, dates from a specific period. Later on we shall try to find an explanation for this paradox in a civilization which, granting nothing to pleasure or to fantasy, ended by organizing the most unseemly and maddest extravagances. But our purpose is not to write a history of these spectacles which lasted for approximately ten centuries. We shall limit ourselves to certain elements which are indispensable for an understanding of the scenes which are to follow.

Because of the almost mythical character which these games have assumed for us, it is difficult for us today to realize to what extent they became one of the most familiar aspects of everyday life. One might even say that they pervaded life. They imposed their rhythm on existence and provided nourishment for the passions. The spectacle was awaited with impatience; everyone discussed it, some applauded and others booed frantically. Goaded by habit, by idleness, by fanaticism, an entire people crowded on to the tiers of the circus or the amphitheatre, as to a temple which had a ritual peculiar to it. In Rome there was undoubtedly an emotion special to the amphitheatre, even as there exists amongst us a quite special pleasure on entering a cinema, regardless of the film which is to be shown. Chateaubriand, in a prose which despite its grandiloquence sometimes retains the authentic colours of life, sought to depict the grandeur and barbarity of these gatherings:

'Meanwhile the masses gathered in the amphitheatre of Vespasian; all Rome rushed to drink the blood of the martyrs. A hundred thousand spectators, some veiled by a corner of their robe, others with a sunshade shielding their head, spread out on the tiers. The mob, erupting from the porticoes, went up and down the outer staircases and took its place on the marble steps. . . . Three thousand bronze statues, a multitude of pictures, columns of porphyry and jasper, precious vases, decorated the scene. . . .

'In a trench dug around the arena a hippopotamus and some crocodiles were swimming; five hundred lions, forty elephants, tigers, panthers, bulls, bears used to tearing men to pieces, roared in the caves of the amphitheatre. Gladiators, no less ferocious, were scattered here and there, wiping their blood-stained arms. Near the dens of the beasts were the places of public prostitution; naked whores and Roman ladies of high society intensified, as in the times of Nero, the horror of the spectacle and, rivals of death, came to dispute the favours of a dying prince. Add the last howlings of the Maenads lying in the streets and breathing their last under the efforts of their god and you will know all the pomps and all the shame of slavery.'

It would be absurd to cavil at Chateaubriand's means of attaining his effects. The historian must concede at least that there was in these gatherings something that exceeded moderation, a sort of barbaric extravagance; but let us hasten to add that behind this imposing setting the inexperienced observer would not take long to discern the routine of the ant-hill.

Before dawn a clamorous and brawling crowd had begun to queue in front of the amphitheatre, waiting for the moment when they would dispute, with blows and jostling, the best places in a sort of 'gods' at the top of the edifice, where the heat could be overpowering. Other spectators, the majority, climbed

(a) Interior of the amphitheatre at Nîmes. The *podium* and the 'ranks' (*maeniana*), where the spectators took their places according to their social status, can be clearly seen. (Photo Jean Dieuzaide)

(b) The greatest of the Roman amphitheatres—the Colosseum. (Photo Boudot-Lamotte)

2. Part of the *cavea* of the amphitheatre at Verona in its present state. The *cunei* are the blocks in the form of wedges marked out by small staircases (*scalaria*) which come down from the vomitories through which the public reached the amphitheatre. (Photo Boudot-Lamotte)

quietly up the steep stairways, a 'ticket' in their hands; they had the right to a place somewhere on the tiers safeguarded by a scrupulous control. They had taken time to refresh themselves, to tidy up, and at the Circus some even hired cushions from the elderly attendant before going to their seats, for one quickly grew stiff sitting on the bare stone. But for the former, riveted to their seats in the 'gods' in fear of losing their places, there was nothing for it but to bring a snack with them; they ate and drank without concern for decorum, even in the presence of the emperor. One day Augustus, through a herald, reproved one of them, telling him that in such circumstances he should go home. The man's answer was: 'Yes, but you do not risk losing your place . . .'.

Nature of the Roman spectacles: the 'games'

In Rome, the spectacles were free—one of the citizens' rights, and not a luxury, to be indulged in or not according to their tastes or means. The city, in short, assured its people their pleasures, even going so far as to organize banquets where anyone could take his seat near the rich or, if he so wished, at the rich man's table. Such a principle implies organization in the strict sense of the word. The spectacles as a whole were regular displays held at fixed intervals throughout the year and were not, if one may so put it, sufficient unto themselves. They depended on an official calendar which fixed the dates of the *ludi*, the games in honour of the gods. It must, however, be added that after a certain date extraordinary spectacles were presented on the initiative of prominent persons, which corresponded more closely, by the very fact that they were given for their own sake, to the idea that we have of them.

Putting aside religious or legal distinctions between games and the relationship between them, we can distinguish six types of spectacle. Of these the chariot races (*ludi circenses*) were by far the most frequent and the most popular. The gladiatorial combats have a rather special place since they were relatively less frequent than the games of the Circus and, for that reason, were appreciated as a special attraction. They were often associated with the *venatio*, the 'hunt' spectacle, a very varied entertainment in which wild animals appeared. It was on this occasion that condemned men were thrown to the beasts. But the *venatio* by no means amounted to that sort of carnage which was considered, even in Roman eyes, as vile and degrading. As well as these spectacles which everyone knows about, there were also two others of a rather special type: the *naumachiae*, which were sea-battles, and those which might be called 'mythological dramas', representations of a very special nature which took place not on the stage but in the amphitheatre.

Finally, the 'games' usually allowed for a number of days set aside for theatrical representations in the real sense. But the theatre, in all its various forms, often very far removed from ours, was a world apart which would require a separate study that cannot be undertaken here.

I

FROM RITE TO SPECTACLE:
THE GLADIATORIAL COMBATS

Beginnings of the gladiatorial combats

The gladiatorial combats first appeared in Rome long after the Circus games, in 264 B.C., as a funerary rite reserved to the aristocracy. That year, indeed, the sons of Junius Brutus, descendants of the great Brutus, decided to honour the memory of their father by matching three pairs of slaves against one another, according to a custom which was not of Roman origin. Though these first gladiators—known as *bustuarii*—derived their name from *bustum*, a word meaning the tomb or the funeral pyre, it does not seem that these combats formed part of the many ceremonies of the funeral itself or that the gladiators fought to the death 'before the tomb' of the dead man, as has sometimes been assumed by a simplification of language. They took place in the days that followed, on a date difficult to state precisely but doubtless, at least at first, on the ninth day after the obsequies, the day which marked the end of the period of mourning after the solemn funeral ceremonies reserved for persons of importance, and on which the funeral games were traditionally celebrated.

The first combat of which we will speak took place in the *forum boarium*, that is to say the cattle-market, but the custom of using the Forum for this kind of display was rapidly established. It had long since ceased to be the 'field of willows and barren reeds' sung by Ovid, or the necropolis watered by a brook which the archaeologists have revealed to us. The stalls of butchers and market-gardeners which at one time bordered the site were no longer there; they had been replaced by those of more noble trades whose façades were decorated with shields captured from the Samnites. These shops, ranged in two ranks, took up one side and the temple of Concord on the other marked off a roughly rectangular arena. The site by this time was embellished by several monuments, whose red-tiled roofs tempered their severity. A sundial brought from Catania was placed near the Rostra, and for another century was destined to show the Romans a slightly incorrect time of day.

Though the setting in which these combats took place had, as we have seen, nothing wild about it, there must have been something rude and primitive about the combats themselves, since there was no preparation, no complicated stage management, to diminish or refine their brutality. Later, someone had the idea of placing seats for hire all round the Forum; but at the beginning the spectators—women were excluded—perched here and there wherever they could find a place, especially on the galleries which had been built above the stalls situated along the edges of the longer sides. Standing upright, and bareheaded, since they had the feeling that they were taking part in a ceremony rather than attending an entertainment, they watched the blood flow among the flagstones of the Forum. The lack of distance conferred a violent and strongly emotional character on the bloodshed—'magic', if you will.

The gladiators fought in couples. At that time they were all armed in the same way, in the 'Samnite' fashion: long, rectangular shield, straight sword, helmet and greaves. We lack, however, any details of the organization of these combats. The historians have only handed down to us the number of pairs summoned to take part; they increase steadily, from three to twenty-five, then from twenty-five to sixty in less than a century. These figures, however, should not make us lose sight of the fact that at this time the gladiatorial combats were totally exceptional in character. Moreover, they were frequently followed by a banquet which was held in the Forum. But it was not because they constituted a munificence in which the populace was invited to share, that these games were known as *munera*; the reason was, according to a tradition handed down to us by Tertullian, that they represented above all an 'obligation' to the dead.

The blood of the shades

Thus, before becoming a spectacle applauded by the dense crowds of the Colosseum, the gladiatorial combats were a rite carried out in recollection of sacred ceremonies. What religious feeling drove the Romans to adopt these macabre games? What savage, archaic rite were they resuscitating, reviving or replacing? They themselves had forgotten—and, moreover, the question no longer preoccupied them. The origin of the combats is obscure. They probably came from Etruria by way of Campania, where, according to Jacques Heurgon, they found 'their full development and classic form' before taking root in Rome. Their exact significance is no less obscure. It has been held that the blood shed by the gladiators was a tribute exacted by those gods, devourers of men, who still dwelt on some of the shores of the Mediterranean. But the texts cited to support this thesis appear to have been dictated, as the late Georges Ville has shown, by Christian propagandists seeking to discredit paganism.

It is wiser to credit the laconic details handed down to us by Festus. 'It was the custom', he writes, 'to sacrifice prisoners on the tombs of valorous warriors; when the cruelty of this custom became evident, it was decided to make gladiators fight before the tomb.' Thus the origin of the combats lay in a softening of customs by which a people still half enslaved to old super-stitions gave, if one may so put it, an orderly form to human sacrifice. The gladiators who took the place of the bound victim played a role similar to that of the reed manikins which were thrown, hands and feet bound, over the Pontus Sublicius on 14 May as a later substitute, no doubt, for living victims. But in the gladiatorial games the effects of this substitution were dramatic rather than symbolic.

The blood of the gladiators was thus shed for the dead. The object was 'to appease their spirits', a convenient, even if ambiguous, formula. It was not intended, it seems, to guard against hostile acts by the dead man or, more specifically, against his always dreaded intrusion into the world of the living. Fear of the dead was undoubtedly far from being alien to Roman religion; in certain circumstances unsatisfied spirits could unchain calamities, of which the worst was to drag the living with them into the other world. But this fear was exorcised by a very exact jurisdiction which limited the return of the *manes* to earth to certain days and defined a host of public and private ceremonies aimed at rendering them inoffensive. The minute detail which in Rome governed the relations of the living and the dead makes it very improbable that the aim of a rite originally reserved to certain privileged persons, and as exceptional as the gladiatorial combats, was to guard against the maleficence of the dead. Above all, the dead man is not by nature an aggressive being who must at all costs be propitiated; the hostility which he harbours is latent and does not become manifest unless the obligatory duties have been neglected—if, for example, he has not been mourned or buried according to the rites. The dead man is, in essence, a shadow emptied of his substance, 'a head without force', indistinct, anonymous. His condition may be defined as a 'lack', a deaf and listless but tenacious quest for a feeling of reality.

What virtue thenceforward can the blood possess, if it is not to set a regeneration in motion and to give the souls which 'sleep' in death a sort of expectation of survival, even if momentary? The blood which flowed between the stones of the Forum and that with which Ulysses held back the souls in the kingdom of Hades at the point of his sword have the same significance. It is only after having drunk that Anticleia, the mother of Ulysses, recognizes her son and speaks to him. The soothsayer Tiresias, moreover, formulates the implacable law which rules the other world; only the souls who drink the blood of the sacrifices will find once more some spark of life and the strength to speak. The others will return to the oblivion from which he would have them emerge. In the end, human blood, spilt in honour of the dead, could assure a permanent revival, that is to say a real deification. It is not surprising if one recalls that the offering of blood is made to warriors and that the gladiatorial combats at Rome, before they became commonplace, were dedicated to their ancestors by members of the great families which, at the end of the Republic, were to invent divine genealogies.

This interpretation, if it is correct, naturally presupposes a foreign influence. We know that the Romans, originally, were so uninterested in the domain of the dead that they, who organized everything, did not try to organize it. All their ceremonies concerning the world beyond were borrowed. It has been said about the Roman religion that 'there is no representation of the domain of the dead or of an after-world in which they live. All that only developed under Greek influence, and partially under Etruscan influence.' Who can be surprised if an imported rite was made a little clearer by an amalgam of alien beliefs?

The rite becomes a spectacle

Luckily for us, it is not in religious history that we must seek the reasons for the exceptional success which the gladiatorial combats were to know. Very soon, even before the end of the Republic, they came to lose their significance as a rite and we can really speak of 'secularization'. Henceforth, in the political life of Rome, they played a precise and specific role for which two factors predestined them.

The first of these was their popularity, which from the very earliest times was great. There was no spectacle that the Romans would not have abandoned in order to attend a gladiatorial combat, except perhaps the chariot races, and even that is not certain; for these, though far more frequent, did not have the prestige conferred upon the *munera* by their comparative rarity. Terence, in any case, proved to his own cost that the public did not hesitate a moment between the cross-talk of his comedies and the sword-play of the gladiators.

The other factor was their private character. This requires some explanation. In the time of the Republic, the state—or the Senate—exercised, at least until the day when its authority became irremediably weakened, a rigorous control over all forms of spectacle. It was the Senate which, within the framework of the religious festivals, fixed the details of a 'calendar of spectacles' whose enforcement was entrusted to the magistrates. A Roman spectacle was a 'public affair', originally at least, for the situation rapidly became more complicated, and the magistrate entrusted with providing entertainment for his fellow citizens was only an executive held in check by strict regulations. The gladiatorial combats alone escaped this control. Until 105 B.C. when it seems they were included among the official spectacles, they were given only by individuals. In theory, anyone could give a spectacle, though it goes without saying that the only people who did so were members of the great families, if only for purely financial reasons; for, even though in second-century Rome the *munera* were of interest to the entire city, the expenses which they involved, and those of the banquet offered to the populace which very frequently followed them, were naturally sustained by the individual who provided them.

Thus left to the initiative of anybody or everybody, these spectacles, by their very popularity, became an ideal instrument of propaganda and publicity for those who dreamed of exceptional careers or striking electoral successes; they afforded an easy method of winning over the plebeians. The Senate, however, was well aware of this. Even at the time when no personal ambition threatened its authority, it was reserved towards the *munera* which flattered the tastes of the 'populace'. Not daring to forbid them or to attack them openly, it did nothing to assure the spectators even the minimum of comfort; we have already seen in what precarious conditions the combats often took place. On several occasions the Senate even took measures to maintain this discomfort. In fact, and this is significant, it was 20 B.C. before Rome was provided with a permanent amphitheatre, in stone, built by Statilius Taurus. Despite these reservations, an innovation destined to have a great future soon made its appearance: a *munus* of exceptional magnificence, the first of a long series, was given not at Rome but at Cartagena by Scipio in honour of his father and his uncle who had been killed in Spain in the struggle against the Carthaginians.

The indecision of Curio and the intuition of Caesar

The gladiatorial combats did not begin to play the role of an electoral propaganda instrument until the disintegration of institutions delivered the state into the hands of the generals aspiring to dictatorship. Ambitious men were not sparing of their favours to the plebeians, who handed out 'credits, commands and appointments', lack of which meant a death sentence to a politician.

The nature of the *munus* became greatly modified. Doubtless its main purpose was always, in principle, to honour the memory of a dead relative. But in fact any pretext was good enough to regale the populace with combats. Caesar even gave one in memory of his daughter, a thing unheard of. As Cicero said: 'To give games is no longer enough to grant stature to the donor.' It became banal. To intensify the spectacle and give it more stability, the custom spread of adding a 'hunt' to the *munus*, and under the Empire it became its usual accompaniment. Knowing how to procure fine tigers therefore became a part of the profession of a politician. In scale the combats themselves bore no relation to those which might have been seen a century before when twenty-five pairs of gladiators took part: Caesar, whom we shall come across continually in connection with this form of publicity, collected more than three hundred pairs for a single *munus*.

The prestige of quantity no longer sufficed. Previously, the plebs had considered this sort of spectacle as a homage rendered by the powerful to their penury—a homage which gave a degree of satisfaction to their sense of justice commensurate with the obligation the morality of ancient times placed upon the rich to leave the crumbs from their table to the disinherited. Now the plebs considered them more or less a right and became captious and particular. They must be dazzled, their pride flattered by splendours. These had to be invented. From this period dates the taste for the 'epic spectacle,' a forerunner of the Hollywood style: thus Caesar, as *aedile*, at the funeral games given in honour of his father, clad his gladiators in silver armour, but this innovation, immediately taken up by L. Murena and C. Antonius soon went out of fashion because of its very success. It soon created no sensation except in the provinces, where a century later Pliny says that it had reached even the most distant *municipium*.

It was this situation which was the source of Curio's difficulties. What could he do to stage a great coup and strike the imagination of the electors, already satiated with 'sensations'? An aggravating circumstance was that Curio was not wealthy and it required colossal wealth to stand such expense. Cicero, deeply hostile not to the games themselves but to the direction which he saw them taking, advised him to give up the idea. Curio paid no heed to the more or less realistic arguments of his correspondent. He borrowed. He then realized that there was still a largely unexplored domain where innovation could achieve a sensation overnight and procure for its author, at a moment's notice, a number of votes which the virtue preached by Cicero would, in the political circumstances of the time, take centuries to assemble. Much attention had indeed been paid to astounding the public by novelties and eccentricities of staging, but, in the middle of the first century B.C., no one had yet considered improving the comfort of the spectators. At this time there did not exist at Rome any permanent edifice specifically designed for gladiatorial combats. They were held in the Circus or, as in the past, in the Forum, where wooden scaffolding was set up for the occasion and then hastily taken away again.

In 53 B.C., therefore, Curio had two wooden theatres built, shaped like a Greek hemicycle and mounted back to back on a pivot. In the morning two different theatrical presentations were given simultaneously; two partitions were sufficient to isolate the two stages and thus prevent the sound of one presentation hampering the other. In the afternoon the two theatres, their tiers crammed with spectators, were swivelled on their pivot: 'and so the whole Roman people', writes Pliny the Elder with a touch of indignation, 'embarked so to speak on two ships, was carried on two pivots'. The two wooden hemicycles joined up, the partitions and the stages were removed and, to the surprise of the amazed Romans, the amphitheatre was born and the gladiators entered the arena.

This formula was over-complicated and had certain other disadvantages, but it led to the idea of erecting in Rome a permanent edifice, such as already existed at Pompeii. This was destined to have a great future. It was a sign of the times that the Curio family did not shine with any especial brilliance; the man had, as Pliny says, 'no other fortune than the discord of the great'. It was, in fact, thanks to the bitterness of political rivalries that he was able to pay back the enormous debts which he had incurred: Caesar paid them in order to attach this man to his cause, and later Curio was able to render him great services. But the very fact that the caprice of a somewhat obscure individual was able to bequeath to Rome the public buildings which it lacked, even though on a temporary basis, shows the extent to which the state had abdicated its responsibilities.

The Senate tried its best to take measures to check this public auction of state posts. But these measures remained more or less a dead letter as far as the games were concerned. While Cicero, in a now famous letter, was using a mixture of allusion and philosophy to express the sneaking irritation and envious irony of a disconsolate and passive aristocracy, Caesar was laying the foundations of what was to be under the Empire an organization obedient to clearly defined principles. He revived and improved the form of the amphitheatre as conceived by Curio, which was to give the gladiatorial combats their final setting right up to the fall of Rome. He paid close attention to the recruitment and training of the gladiators. Suetonius says that he issued an order that any well-known gladiator who failed to win the approval of the public should be forcibly rescued from execution and reserved for the coming show. New gladiators were trained not by the usual professionals but by Roman knights and even senators skilful in the art. . . . Caesar even had a gladiatorial school built at Ravenna. In fact he created, at least in embryo, the amphitheatre and the imperial *ludi*, realizing that it was necessary to endow the authorities with the means of contenting a mob ever more greedy for this kind of spectacle.

Imperial policy

It only remained for the emperors to learn the lessons of experience. They hastened to appropriate, to their own advantage, as far as they could, a means of propaganda whose efficacy was to be proved by history. The organization which thenceforward controlled the right to give *munera* showed a more and more open tendency to monopoly, which was expressed by legislative measures and considerations of fact; in Rome at least all the gladiatorial combats, with the exception of those held in December, were offered to the people by the emperor. It was he who determined their scope, their duration and their date. Generally speaking, he chose to celebrate them on exceptional occasions: anniversaries, inaugurations, victories. But this was not an absolute rule: Suetonius reports that Caligula improvised a *munus* at the request of some loafers. This whim illustrates their real character clearly enough. The imperial *munera* were really 'at the ruler's will'.

We cannot be certain that individuals or magistrates were actually forbidden to give *munera*, and one or two instances of their doing so are cited in the annals of the Empire. But what man of any prominence would have risked awaking, by means of an extremely costly liberality, the suspicions of a power which was often unhealthily jealous and quick to exile or suppress those it saw as rivals? And to flatter the populace openly by lavishing on it a spectacle in which it delighted was to set oneself up as just such a rival. Certainly, in provincial cities the central power had not the same reasons to become suspicious. That a magistrate of Nîmes or Antioch should win his right to the recognition of his fellow citizens and a reputation for generosity by providing an extravagant or exceptional *munus* could never offend the emperor. Nor did anything hinder such a citizen from earning his right to a statue by bequeathing to his city, as was done at Thessaloniki, the sums needed for the celebration of a *munus*. But the nature of the legislation in force in such a case, whatever it may have been, is unimportant. For throughout the Empire the gladiatorial combats were for the most part given by the high priests of the imperial cult, provincial or municipal, and were dedicated not to the dead, as they had been formerly, but to the emperor, about whose person all the religious feeling aroused by the spectacles would crystallize. Thus on these particularly impressive occasions the master of the Empire was symbolically present for the people at the four corners of the Roman world. Let us add that he was also present through the niggling regulations which fixed the number of days for the rejoicings and even the number of gladiators who could take part.

This rigid control, which tended to paralyse the initiative of individuals and of magistrates, would have had the disadvantage, had the principle been logically applied, of reducing the number of *munera;* but because of their popularity it was necessary to ensure that they were held frequently. From this arose another aspect of imperial policy, in contradiction to the first: the concern for frequency drove the emperor in certain circumstances to renounce the privilege of offering this largesse to the populace in favour of the magistrates. Thus we note that throughout the Empire the provincial high priests were obliged to provide *munera*. At Rome it was the praetors, and then the quaestors, who had this responsibility; every year, in the month of December, they had to celebrate a *munus*, which was distinguished from those given by the emperor by its regularity and its rigid character.

But—and it is here that the subtlety of the system becomes apparent—the number of pairs which the magistrates could provide in the course of these spectacles was rigorously limited, so much so that by comparison with the *munera* given by the emperor, the splendour and luxury of which sometimes exceeded the limits of the probable, they played the modest role of a sort of daily bread. Their propaganda value was correspondingly reduced. The state, while assuring the plebs 'their' annual *munus*, thus cut the grass from under the feet of the ambitious.

This system had other advantages. The public treasury was freed from expenses which would otherwise have weighed heavily upon it, for the charges were naturally borne by the magistrates. For them, within the framework of the authoritarian regime, the annual *munera* ended by being no more than a costly obligation, a tax on rank and honours, which, in the last days of the Empire, the magistrates tried their best to avoid.

The organization of Domitian

Quite apart from the enormous expenses of the 'hunt' which usually accompanied them, the gladiatorial combats were expensive, sometimes indeed very expensive, owing to the quality of the men engaged: the veterans of the arena, experts in their profession and famous for their victories, represented, as we shall see, a real capital which a sword-blow could destroy. This was inevitable since, without loss of men, a *munus* would have had no attraction. Similarly with the number of combatants in the lists: Augustus produced, on an average, 625 pairs of gladiators for each spectacle. To celebrate his victory over the Dacians, Trajan made 10,000 men fight, many of whom, it is true, must have been unskilled prisoners. How was the human troupe for such colossal spectacles obtained?

At one time, the donor stuffed his purse and went to the *lanista*. This was a picturesque individual who provided the *editor* (the 'producer', if you will, but with this essential difference that he financed the spectacle without the slightest hope of recouping the smallest part of the monies involved) with the gladiators he needed. The *lanista* expected to reap a considerable profit from the sale or rent of the troupe which he had trained in his barracks.

He was, in fact, in the position of an all-powerful go-between, for the magistrates dared not be stingy; they would be discredited if they presented spavined gladiators to the public. The *lanista*, therefore, easily imposed his scale of charges. It was enough for him to speculate on the urgency of the need whenever gladiators—and good ones—had to be found. But the financial advantages which he drew from his lucrative enterprise were balanced by the social and moral degradation to which he was subject. He was ranked, like the meanest of his gladiators, with the most vile and infamous. In the eyes of the Romans he was regarded as both a butcher and a pimp. He played the role of scapegoat; it was upon him that society cast all the scorn and contempt aroused by an institution which reduced men to the status of merchandise or cattle.

Curiously enough this scorn was not felt for those who maintained a troupe of gladiators at their own expense and traded in them, since that was not their normal means of existence but only a subsidiary source of income. According to law, moreover, any citizen had the right to maintain a troupe whose importance was not, in principle, limited. The magistrates, urged on by the credit which they sought to obtain, prided themselves from the first century onward, on their obligations and possessed their own troupes, which they were free to hire out if they had no immediate use for them.

Again the Empire had only to systematize an already rich experience. The magnificence of the *munera* which it provided did not allow it to rely upon middlemen. The state became a contractor; it set up barracks, the imperial *ludi*, which in Rome were the only authorized schools of gladiators. Thus legal privilege was coupled with economic semi-monopoly.

Other than the *Ludus Matutinus*, where the 'hunters' who were to fight with wild beasts were trained, there were three of these *ludi*: the *Ludus Gallicus*, the *Ludus Dacicus* and the *Ludus Magnus*. This last—the exact location of which in Rome was uncertain until, in 1937, the excavations began which were to reveal its substantial remains—was quite close to the Colosseum with which it was linked (or so it seems) by an underground passage, as Colini and Cozza have shown in their publication on the *Ludus Magnus*. Its construction, begun by Domitian, was completed by Trajan and Hadrian. Under Marcus Aurelius it was destroyed by fire, but it was quickly repaired, since it was one of the buildings indispensable to the community.

We shall describe elsewhere the daily routine of these grim places. Their organization alone interests us here. They were vast and included, other than the cells and training grounds, an arsenal and a forge. They employed a full staff, from armourers to trainers, to say nothing of a doctor. To control this autarchic institution a whole hierarchy of officials was needed, having at its head a *procurator* responsible for the technical and financial administration; his importance is shown by the fact that he belonged to the equestrian order.

Rome, however, had no monopoly of imperial barracks; there were others in all the provinces, at Praeneste, at Capua, at Alexandria, at Pergamon. These were usually of less importance; a single official assumed control of several barracks in the same area. Thus one was *procurator per Gallias, per Asiam*, etc. These establishments, it must be stressed, were not intended solely to supply the needs of the provinces. They were seed-beds whence was recruited the elite called upon to appear at Rome in the imperial *munera*.

It is rather difficult to form an idea of the number of gladiators that the barracks were able to maintain. Perhaps, for those in Rome itself, up to 2,000 men. But when compared with the scope of this widespread organization, the *lanista* henceforth seemed more or less an artisan. The greater part of the market escaped him; in the provinces, even if some high priests applied to him to find gladiators, others had their own troupes. Even more, from the times of Marcus Aurelius, the state not only imposed on him fixed charges but obliged him to supply to every organizer of a *munus* a certain number of gladiators at a low price. Thus the market for gladiators became a closed one, more or less shackled by regulations based on the principle that 'the production of *munera* is a matter of public interest'.

It only remained for the new regime to create a framework commensurate with the combats which it provided. The Republic, as we have seen, had bequeathed only the general idea. Its

panied by an orchestra, which sometimes marked their stages. Mosaic from the villa at Zliten, Tripoli Museum. (Photo Boudot-Lamotte)

4(b) A Roman lamp. The gladiato[r] on the right is a Thracian; he i[s] wielding the *sica* and wearing hig[h] greaves which protect part of hi[s] thigh. His adversary is a 'big shiel[d] man. Vienne Museum (Isère). (Museu[m] photo)

4(a) Bronze figure of a gladiator, found at Lillebonne (Seine-Maritime). He is wearing the *subligaculum*, a sort of quilted tunic, greaves and the *manica* on his sword-arm. His left arm and torso are protected by the shield. Musée des Antiquités, Rouen. (Photo Ellebé)

4(c) A fighting scene on a Roman lamp. The Thracian threatens his adversary who continues to fight despite the loss of his shield. Vienne Museum. (Museum photo)

realization was preceded by several anarchic or unfortunate attempts. The first permanent amphitheatre was due to the initiative of an immensely rich individual, Statilius Taurus, on the instigation if not under the aegis of Augustus, who was a personal friend, but the building was destroyed in the great fire which devastated Rome under Nero. The Empire had to return to the old formula of improvised wooden amphitheatres which were dismantled after the spectacle, or which at best were sufficiently solidly constructed to last for several years, like that of Nero. The problem was not solved till the end of the first century A.D. by Vespasian, who began the construction of the Colosseum, which was completed by his successors Titus and Domitian. An immense labour force had to be got together to complete so enormous a task in a comparatively short time. The travertine used in the construction was brought from the Tiber quarries, about seventeen miles from Rome. A road was specially built for this purpose, along which, according to tradition, 30,000 Jewish prisoners assigned to the task formed an uninterrupted double line. In the circumstances, the idea of a Caesar-Pharoah was no fantasy. The monument, in fact, was of grandiose proportions.

A city on tiers

On the eve of the day when games out of the ordinary were to be given, the population of the city was swelled by a multitude of Italians and foreigners, advised of the event by placards placed on the tombs along the verges of the main roads. The rich left their country houses and the peasants their flocks. Rome, already over-populated, could not lodge all these sightseers and took on the appearance of a camp. Tents were set up in the streets on the flint paving and at the crossroads, near the sanctuaries of the Lares; the throng was such that men lost their lives, crushed or suffocated.

But the following day, when the spectacle was about to begin, the city was totally abandoned to the philosophers and the thieves. There were no strollers on the Campus Martius and no visitors on these dead days which Seneca, in some celebrated passages, took pleasure in using as a backcloth to some of his meditations. Nothing, he said, came to disturb the absolute peace of the solitary thinker save that, from time to time, 'a sudden, a universal, burst of applause' shook the silent city and reverberated as far as the hills caparisoned in deep green. But these cries did not disturb him; they may have given him the idea of the theory of the parallelism between body and soul which does not concern us here; or perhaps he ignored them for 'the confused rumbling of a crowd is like the waves, like the wind which whips the forest, like everything which conveys only unintelligible sounds'.

As for the innumerable gradations of thieves who pullulated in Rome, it was necessary to prevent them from profiting by the occasion, pincers and jemmies in hand, and to station city guard-posts for the duration of the spectacle.

About 60,000 persons took their seats for the hunts and combats in the Flavian amphitheatre, where several coins of the imperial epoch show them assembled. One of these is valuable as a symbol; in naive style it portrays, seated in the midst of his people, the emperor Gordian the Pious, whose silhouette is set in bold relief to the exclusion of all other material details which might force themselves on the attention. Another, minted under Titus, is a bronze commemoration medal on which the Colosseum appears as if seen from a distant and dominating height; on the tiers visible in the lower level of the façade, reproduced with the greatest precision, the packed throng is like a fan. Two unbroken staircases, starting almost at the topmost gallery and converging inevitably on the arena, stress the absolute uniformity: 'everywhere the same aspect, nothing to break the continuity of the seats, nothing standing out'.

It is possible to admire 'this equality of places which seems to confound the ruler with the people', which Pliny complimented Trajan for introducing. But it was no more than a demagogic fiction and, at the amphitheatre even more than at the circus, social inequality was translated with a precision the greater the more the edifices grew in importance and complexity. A stranger seeing it at closer range, or entering by one of the four doors giving on to the suite above the arena, would have been aware of this at first glance by the simple contrast between the white togas which adorned the tiers up to about two-thirds of the height of the building and the dark garments of the common people crammed high up between a dividing wall decorated with statues and the columns of the covered gallery. In fact, the *cavea*, that is to say all the tiers where the spectators took their seats, was divided by three circular walls (*baltei*) into four super-imposed sections, of which the highest (*pullati*) included a sub-division; there were thus five categories of seats in all.

The first, or *podium*, was made up of four ranks of tiers im-mediately above the arena and surrounded by two walls whose magnificence caught the eye. The upper one (the first *balteus*) which separated the *podium* from the rest of the *cavea* was decorated with mosaics; the other—the front wall—thirteen feet high, designed to isolate the spectators from the arena, was entirely of marble. This material as well as being impressive had the advantage of affording no foothold for the wild beasts. During the 'hunts', moreover, there were additional safety measures. Another peculiarity of the *podium* was that it had wider tiers than the other parts; these were designed to accom-modate the chairs with which persons of distinction with reserved seats—senators, vestals, senior magistrates, etc.—mindful of their comfort, provided themselves. It was also in the *podium* that the emperor's box was situated near the entry on the lesser axis of the arena, whence, in consequence, the best view was obtained. The box was entered by special staircases which made it possible, should the need arise, to leave the spectacle unobserved, whereas opposite to it, on the same axis, was another box reserved for the consuls and the president of the games. A detail from Suetonius suggests that some of the dignitaries were not averse to diversify-ing the uniformity of the white togas by adding a splash of colour to their clothes. But this was sometimes at peril of their lives; Caligula did not hesitate to order the execution of a King

35

of Egypt, his guest and his cousin, whose purple mantle created a sensation at the games. In the circumstances, it was not entirely a touch of sheer madness; the people kept their eyes fixed on the *podium* and the least detail was of significance, so much so that Augustus in his wisdom considered it preferable that Claudius, because of his strange appearance, should never sit beside him in the imperial box.

Above the *podium* rose two ranks of tiers separated by a wall (the second *balteus*). The first of these was reserved for the knights and the second for the tribunes and citizens. There was not, it seems, any great difference between these two sections, known as the first and second *maenianum;* the sole privilege according the knights was the use of a cushion. On the other hand, the last *balteus,* between the second and third *maenianum,* represented, one might say, a very definite distinction, the boundary of that part of the edifice reserved for the patricians. It was decorated with statues alternating with columns and pierced by doors giving access to the *cavea*. Behind it sat the poor, those who had not the status of citizen, in patched mantles fastened by clumsy brooches, their footwear gaping open to reveal the coarse thread with which the rents had been freshly cobbled—and the slaves. The right to attend the spectacles on the tiers of the second *maenianum* was a privilege, like the dole of food, accorded to citizenship. Higher up, the wooden tiers of the covered gallery which crowned the amphitheatre were for the women.

To avoid all disorder and to allow the crowd to take their places without inconvenience there was a double system of communications: one, horizontal, was formed by the corridors (*praecinctiones*) which, along each dividing wall, encircled the arena; the second, vertical, by little staircases (*scalaria*) which, starting from each of the open doors in the third *balteus*, converged between the tiers towards the *podium*, dividing the *cavea* into equal sections known as *cunei*, since they had the form of a wedge.

This abstract classification may well suggest to the reader an atmosphere which was not precisely that of the gatherings in the Colosseum. Here one must almost inevitably evoke the Rome of the satirists, so true was it that the senators in the places of honour were far from all being Catos, nor had the knights much in common with the men who, two centuries earlier, had followed the generals to make their fortune in semi-pacified countries at risk of life and limb. Of the latter Juvenal was relentless in boldly painting the blackest of portraits: only 'former employees of the municipal arenas with puffy cheeks already well known to the public', sons of pimps and *lanistas*, and gigolos who had found the way to wealth and fortune by 'the surest method available today, the vulva of some rich old woman', had the right to applaud from these seats.

Let us pass over the shame and the vices of these men. Their appearance will suffice. Their fingers dripping sweat and grease, despite the countless attentions they paid to their skin, were covered with rings set with precious stones which they did not wear on the right hand like the ancient Romans but on the left, for fear lest they might be damaged. When they placed their hands on their heads, it was on bald skulls that all this jewellery glistened, for with an affectation of Stoicism they shaved their skulls and let their beards grow. This led Juvenal to say that 'they have hair shorter than an eyebrow'. Others did not hesitate to dye their hair or to wear wigs. Is it strange that in the gait and in the faces of these men there was something of the charlatan and the urchin? The gladiator handling his net in the arena had more noble blood in his veins than all the senators assembled there, more even than the ruler himself who donated the games. Consider, moreover, how Caligula appeared in public: in the costume of Venus, or with the boots of a messenger or a woman's buskins, or dressed in the cuirass of Alexander the Great which he had had specially excavated from his tomb and which he embellished with the badges of his triumphs—which for him meant no more than a cravat.

As for the wives of these dignitaries, to whom was reserved the honour of sitting near the Vestals, it must be asked if they came to the amphitheatre to see or to be seen. They arrived in a litter, half-veiled 'so as not to provoke glances', carried by eight trotting Syrian slaves whose muscles throbbed under their red liveries and preceded by African runners in white tunics. From this walking palace emerged a blonde who until the sixth hour had been a brunette—but the Germans were fashionable then— and the scaffolding of her hair was as complex as the ground plan of the Colosseum. She wore a fortune in jewellery, bracelets weighing ten pounds, set with gems one of which alone would have sufficed to buy half Italy. But Ogulnia's fortune had been hired, as had all the rest—robe, escort, friends, nurse and waiting-maid—all hired for this great day. Only the rouge, plastered in layers on her face, came from her own cupboard.

Something of this everyday scandal must surely have been evident on the tiers of the Colosseum; but in action rather than appearance, in person rather than clothing. In such a case we may assume that the women left to the care of their maid-servants those little tame snakes with which they sometimes adorned their necks on the pretext of cooling them, and that the queers left on the pegs in their wardrobes those transparent tunics in which certain of them did not blush to plead their cause. For the religious character of the games, even though the spectators had no more than a vague recollection of it, imposed at least certain rules of decency and prohibited the more flagrant excesses—the appanage of eccentric emperors and their favourites. But one must not exaggerate the degradation of the senate and the equestrian order. It was only too true that just at the time when the Colosseum was being built Vespasian augmented the ranks of the knights decimated by the exactions of the Julio-Claudian dynasty by the mass admission of knights who did not always have a brilliant social background. Even if everyone paraded the haughtiness of parvenus, the degradation with which Juvenal taxes them is, to a certain extent, due also to rhetorical exaggeration and class prejudice.

At the moment of which we write the attention of the spectators was divided between the excitement caused by new arrivals and the programme (*libellus numerarius*) which they had bought in the street. This contained the names of the gladiators who were to fight in the afternoon combats, but not who was to fight whom. And it was precisely this question of who would be matched with this or that champion which enlived the conversation and created excitement, discussion and betting.

The route of a latecomer

While the crowd on the tiers awaited the appearance of the procession, the last spectators would be making their way towards the entries across the travertine esplanade where only just now the crowd had been jostling and which, flanked by pillars, now looked like a deserted plinth from which the mass of the Colosseum loomed. 'I have seen', says the peasant of Calpurnius, 'an amphitheatre formed by an assemblage of colossal beams, which rises to the skies and seems to look upward to the Tarpeian rock. . . . Even as a mountain chain, forested on all its sides, embraces a valley in its sinuous contours. . . .'

Yet this stunned astonishment on the part of provincials or strangers—a source of amusement and ill-concealed pride to the Romans—was not at seeing this type of monument, for many cities, even small ones, had such buildings; nor was it due to the particularly imposing dimensions of the Colosseum. A great number of amphitheatres, in fact, had been built in the most ingenious manner possible, with the evident intention of making use of local resources. If they had not been entirely cut out of the rock as at Sutri, or placed on the flanks of a ravine where the water-course had been turned aside, many were cut into the slope of a mountain or hill terraced around the periphery of a depression. This was so especially at Paestum, at Pozzuoli and at Pompeii. This system—which was not the rule in all the provinces, as is proved by the striking exceptions of the arenas of Arles and Nîmes, which will be discussed later—made it possible to effect great economies, since it simplified the problems of balance and proportion and reduced by an equivalent amount the volume of sub-construction necessary to adapt the

39

site more perfectly to the design of the building to be constructed; at Paestum, for example, only the upper part caused any difficulty, the lower tiers being excavated straight out of the soil.

But if economics gained by such artifices, aesthetics did not. For the amphitheatre, dominated by the mass of the heights lowering over it, and often swallowed up by the mass of buildings surrounding it, had no character other than that of a utilitarian edifice more or less obliterated by the town of which it formed a part.

The Colosseum, on the other hand, built in the ancient hollow where the Golden House of Nero had formerly stood, between the Velian, the Caelian and the Esquiline, on a site which the Flavian architects had drained, filled in and consolidated, rose sheer in complete isolation and at once asserted itself as a public building. In order properly to appreciate its grandiose appearance it should also be remembered that its exterior was not, as it is today, a dull grey, but a uniform white whose brilliance was emphasised by the dark shadows of the arcades. For travertine, brought from Tiber, was used in this part of the building. Care had also been taken lest a too uniform decoration should diminish the general effect. The façade was made up of four storeys, with differing orders, in which Doric, Ionic and Corinthian were successively superimposed. The first three were embellished by eighty half-engaged columns alternating with an equal number of arcades; between the Ionic and Corinthian columns of the second and third orders, three feet in diameter, were statues about twenty feet tall, on pedestals; they were free-standing full-length figures which stood out from the shadows of the arcades, set at regular intervals in two superimposed ranks round the whole circumference of the edifice to break the monotony of the stone. The arcade over the entrance used by the emperor was distinguished by a quadriga and free-standing columns. The fourth order consisted of a solid wall, decorated not by columns but by simple pilasters, between which forty small rectangular windows alternated with an equal number of round bucklers (*clipei*), perhaps placed there by Domitian. Above each window three corbels supported masts which showed above the roof of the edifice and served to hold up the *velarium* intended to protect the spectators from the sun.

The first order had no ornament other than the eight columns alternating with the arcades which all served as entries to the amphitheatre. Four of them, situated at the extremities of the major and minor axes, were reserved for the gladiators, the emperor and the *editor*, the president of the games.

It was towards one of the seventy-six others, intended for common mortals, that the spectator made his way. But he did not choose it haphazardly; each bore on the keystone of its vault a number, which one can still see engraved there today. He held in his hand a counter which, like those which gave a right to the distribution of wheat, had been given him free. Various types have been found, all of which, undoubtedly, were for the games. Some, and these are the rarest, are real tickets bearing the number of a *cuneus*, of a tier, and even the precise indication of a seat: *Cun VI In(feriori) (gradu decimo) VIII*, that is to say Cuneus 6, lower tier No. 10, place No. 8; and, in this case, the spectator knew which arcade corresponded to the seat in question. But most of them only bore on their surface scenes relating to the games—gladiators, charioteers, animals—or very vague indications mentioning for which type of spectacle they were valid, for example LUD (I)—Games, or DIES VENAT(ionis)—Days of the Hunt. It has been supposed quite reasonably that the mass of spectators in the amphitheatre sat by tribes, each one of which had its particular counters which, apart from giving the right of entry, probably directed the bearer automatically to a specific section of the *cavea*. The purpose of the numbers engraved on the arcades becomes indeed obscure, without a definite system for seating the people, made the more necessary by the need to seat 50,000 spectators in a relatively short time.

If he arrived from the north-west, the spectator would have passed in front of the colossus of Nero, a statue one hundred feet high, which changed its face every quarter of a century at the caprice or the megalomania of the emperors; it was half embedded in the façade. Some yards farther on he ascended a staircase of exceptional steepness from which covered walks, called *ambulacra,* led right and left into the blocks. Leaving behind him the second and third *ambulacrum,* which gave access respectively to the *podium* and the first *maenianum,* he continued to climb in the half-light—it was the arcades of the second and third order which gave light to the staircases—up to the second, where he found the *vomitoria* which served the *maenianum* where he was to take his seat; these were openings which, throughout the amphitheatre, gave access to the little stairs which cut the tiers into sections. But he need not have climbed as high as that. Other vomitories, mere openings made in the central part of the *maenianum,* opened directly on to the tiers. Then, in the geometrical recess of the balustrade, decorated with scrolls, his hand resting on one of the leaping hares which marked the slope, he came into view right in the midst of the swarming crowd which we described earlier at the foot of the same little staircase, where a *locarius,* or usher, took charge of him.

The final minutes

From the time of the Republic, these minutes of waiting, punctuated by the arrival of the most prominent politicians of the day, gave the crowd the opportunity to show its feelings, an opportunity which it did not let slip, and the appearance of this or that personage could unchain enthusiasm or a chorus of catcalls almost equivalent to a riot. On some days, after the announcement of a particularly popular *senatus-consultus,* the whole gathering burst into applause for the Senate. The ovations redoubled every time a senator entered the enclosure, and when the consul who was giving the games finally appeared the mass of spectators rose and acclaimed him, hands stretched out towards him. Clodius, on the other hand, who arrived at the games by alleys and by-ways, slipped into his seat, and his head appeared suddenly among the crowd like a gate-crasher in a queue; as soon as he was recognised the boos and shouts were such that the gladiators started involuntarily and the horses whinnied with fear. That Cicero, to whom we owe this anecdote, should for personal reasons have given a portrait of him that is virtually a caricature hardly matters. There were cases when a man who had incurred great disfavour was literally chased by the spectators, and it was well known that a claque, with whistles, various missiles or applause at the word of command, tried to arouse the emotions of the crowd.

In the time of the Empire nothing remained of this save the applause; the claque had become, so to speak, an official institution. There were sometimes, indeed, demonstrations hostile to the authorities but, as far as we know, these were exceptional. When the emperor entered, all the spectators rose and acclaimed him standing. His arrival was one of the ceremonial moments preceding the games. Another was the moment when the gladiators entered the arena with great pomp, dressed in gold-embroidered chlamides and purple stuffs, surrounded by a procession (*pompa*) recalling the religious origin of the games.

We do not know exactly what was the protocol for the prelude to the games. Perhaps the gladiators, on entering, made the circuit of the arena, and passing before the emperor's box addressed him with the greeting which has become famous: *Ave, Caesar, morituri te salutant*. One may also assume that there was a second procession, distinct from the first, which probably took place after the distribution of arms and in the course of which the gladiators would have intoned that fateful greeting. In any case, we know that, between their ceremonial entry and the first fight, two events of the greatest importance took place: the drawing of lots and the inspection of arms.

The total number of gladiators who had to appear in the spectacle was decided in advance; but none of the programmes which we have found mentions the composition of the 'pairs' called upon to fight. This was, it seems, decided at the last moment by drawing lots in public. This was presided over by the *editor* in person, probably to avoid fraudulent practices to which the existence of 'factions' could easily have given rise. The public, indeed, and the emperor had their favourites whom they supported passionately. Some were partisans of the 'small shields' like Caligula who swore only by the 'Thracians', others of the 'large shields', and bets were laid on the issue of the combats.

It seems probable that in this drawing of lots account was taken of the special skill and experience of the gladiators called upon to appear in the same performance. There would have been no point in opposing a veteran of the arena and some novice who had not yet had even a single victory. Furthermore, the gladiator himself would have judged it dishonourable to be paired with an adversary not of his stature. A humorous drawing found on the walls of Pompeii appears to be an illustration *ad absurdum* of this rule: one of the gladiators depicted, a *retiarius* called Antigonus, claimed 2,112 victories—a figure which may have been reached by a charioteer, but which is quite absurd for a gladiator. His adversary, Superbus, had only one. A framed caption to the drawing attributes to the *lanista,* represented alongside the two combatants, the word which it is hard not to charge with irony: 'Approach!'.

The *probatio armorum* or arms inspection entrusted to the *editor,* that is to say sometimes the emperor himself, who occasionally delegated it to some distinguished guest, in principle also aimed at excluding any irregularity liable to falsify the outcome of the combat. But we may ask ourselves if this was not also to satisfy the spectators who wished to be assured that everything was in order; for it consisted mainly in making sure that the cutting edge of the weapons was perfectly sharp. Drusus, the son of Tiberius, for example, ruthlessly rejected them if they had the slightest fault, so much so that his name was given to a particularly murderous type of sword.

While all this was going on the gladiators who remained in the arena gave a foretaste of their skill by devoting themselves to various warming-up exercises which spared them the nervousness of suspense. Some, throwing their shields in the air, tried to catch them again in the most fantastic manner, or amused themselves by making borrowed javelins execute elegant movements; but for the most part they practised their attack, and thrust and parried with blunted arms. Sometimes amateurs joined them in the arena to have their skill admired.

Finally, when these practice arms had been exchanged for combat weapons which the president had finished examining, the trumpets sounded the signal for the real encounter.

II

IN THE ARENA

Duels with well-established rules

The first gladiators took their stand in the middle of the stretch of sand ninety-two yards by fifty-seven which formed the arena, frail silhouettes overwhelmed by the enormous surging crowd swarming on the tiers. Their helmets, which entirely covered their faces, first caught the eye; they rivalled each other in excessive weight and complexity. But other than that the two men differed completely in appearance: one, whose body apart from his chest was covered with pieces of metal and leather, carried a small shield in his left hand; the other, almost naked, held a rounded, oblong shield which, seen from the front, completely covered him so that only his head and feet were visible. The first belonged to the class of gladiators known as Thracians, whose appearance at Rome dated from the time of Sulla. He wore a red *subligaculum*, a sort of loin-cloth supported at the waist by a sword-belt (*balteus*). Both legs were protected by metal half-cylinders (*ocreae*) fixed against the tibia and covering a small portion of the hip. His left arm was covered by a *manica*, a sort of leathern sleeve reinforced by metal scales, of which one, at the lower end, protected the upper part of his hand, leaving only the fingers uncovered. His offensive weapon was not one of those strange swords bent almost at right angles in the centre with which the Thracian sometimes fought. It was a fairly short sabre known as a *sica*, curved in the manner of a scythe.

The other gladiator was one of those known in the days of Augustus as Samnites and later as *hoplomachi*, either because it might have seemed insulting to apply to gladiators the name of a people which had for a long time formed part of the Latin community, or because this class had practically disappeared, becoming split into two more specialized types of gladiator: the *secutor*, the usual adversary of the *retiarius*, and the *hoplomachus*, who was matched with the Thracian. It was indeed rare for two gladiators of similar class to fight each other. Each man had his own means of defence and his own technique, differing from that of his adversary, and it was this that partly provided the interest of a combat whose principle consisted just as much in matching two types of weapon as in matching two men. Thus the *hoplo-machus* was deprived of those complicated trappings which his adversary wore, since the exceptional height of his shield—which differentiated him from his predecessor, the Samnite, whose shield was not so large—already assured him sufficient protec-tion; other than the loin-cloth, he wore only an *ocrea* on the left leg and leather bands (*fasciae*) on the wrists, the knee and the ankle of the other, unprotected, leg.

Solidly planted on his legs, his body a little tensed, the *hoplomachus* watched; awaiting a favourable moment, he kept his shield close to his chest with such force that his movements seemed more aggressive than protective. His right hand was pressed against the hilt of his sword whose point was flush with the edge of his shield so that his body offered to his adversary only a single line, and when the Thracian, carrying his shield horizon-tally at the level of his chin and holding his *sica* against his hip, rushed at him, he avoided the attack by a slight sideways move-ment of his whole body. The crowd, fascinated, murmured in appreciation and, remembering that the small shield men were not usually the victors, already foresaw the defeat of the Thracian by the mastery of this parry.

But this was no more than a prelude; the arms now clashed in longer encounters, in the course of which each of the men parried and attacked several times. Feints, attacks, skilful with-drawals followed one another; it was the left side of the body which was the most frequently exposed for, because of the shield, it was more open to attack, as in fencing, which was why the gladiator with only one greave wore it on his left leg. But despite the fierceness of the combat the two gladiators scarcely moved from their pitch; both had many times been victors and experience had taught them to avoid unnecessary movement. The *hoplomachus* could be seen to crouch, flex his arm and place his sword ready to thrust on the rim of his shield wedged against his left knee; or with his shield hugging his body from chin to feet like an apron fall upon his adversary with drawn sword. Such regular movements did not characterize the Thracian. In the words of the Greek writer Artemidorus of Ephesus, he skimmed into the attack, sometimes throwing his whole body to the right as if to mow down the *hoplomachus* with his curved weapon, sometimes lifting his shield far in front of him on a level with his eyes so as to leave his weapon free for an upward thrust. At these times his blade flitted in short zig-zags while his shield see-sawed until it covered his arms almost horizontally, so much so that its inner face, with its fastening strap, became visible for several moments. It sometimes also happened that the two men confronted each other in an absolutely symmetrical position like two cats face to face.

But however great the part played by skill and technique, there was also the question of endurance which enabled a man 'to last out the day and resist the scorching sun in the midst of the burning dust, drenched all the while with his own blood', or prevented him from doing so. Owing to excessive weariness, or possibly because he stumbled against something, or because the blow struck by his adversary had thrown him off balance or seriously injured him, the Thracian fell. In earlier days this would not have been pardoned. The emperor Claudius, in fact, hurriedly turning down his thumb before the crowd was able to show its feelings, used to have the throats cut even of those gladiators who had fallen by accident.

As soon as he tottered there was a unanimous shout from the tiers: '*Habet! Hoc habet!*' ('He's had it!') among which could be heard soon afterwards a very few cries of '*Mitte!*' ('Send him

5(*a*) The death-blow. The loser is a *retiarius*; he does not wear a helmet. Sculpture in ivory at the Roman Museum at Avenches (Switzerland). (Photo Bersier, Fribourg)

5(*b*) Small bronze of a gladiator. Lectoure Museum (Gers). (Photo ciné Barbé)

(b)

(a)

6(a) The trident threatens the left leg of the *secutor* (right), well protected by its greave (*ocrea*), while his right arm which must be thrust forward to reach his adversary is covered by the *manica*. The *galerus*, a piece of metal fixed to the left shoulder of the *retiarius*, shields him from lateral blows.

6(b) The *paegniarii*. Mosaic from the villa at Nennig. See Chapter II. (Photo State Conservatory, Saarbrücken)

back!'), for the Thracian, whose fall had not been a bad one, continued to fight one hand behind him on the ground to hold himself up, his body arched to keep his enemy at a distance. This courageous attitude aroused the pity of some of the spectators who had thought him already beaten, a view he did not share. He was back on his feet with a bound, making a sign of vigorous denial to the crowd to show that he had not yet 'had it' or scorn of the pity shown him. The combat was renewed but with a different rhythm. The *hoplomachus*, encouraged by the crowd, pressed his adversary, who no longer seemed so sure on his feet and was soon driven back against the wall of the *podium* where he restricted himself to parrying blows.

Suddenly the Thracian broke away, threw aside his shield, raised one finger of his left hand towards the spectators, in token of his inability to continue the combat, and begged for their clemency. His outstretched arm streamed with blood which dripped on to his greave, making furrows which mingled with the arabesques that decorated it; above his left breast another wound, which had till then been masked by his shield, spouted blood. The *hoplomachus*, his sword still threatening, stood motionless and turned towards the box of the *editor*, the president of the games, who happened to be the emperor himself; it was the *editor* who, in principle, decided whether the beaten man would be sent back safe and sound (*missus*) or put to death on the spot.

To be sure, certain emperors, when they gave the games, did not scruple to abuse this right. One could cite many examples resulting from cruelty; Claudius, for instance, had every defeated *retiarius* systematically killed because as they did not wear helmets they died with their faces exposed, and the course of their death agony could be followed; or from partisan passions in favour of one or other of the factions of the great or little shields, or from a kind of macabre humour, as when Caracalla once replied to the gladiator who was appealing for his life: 'Go and ask your adversary.' But most frequently the *editor* would share the views of the crowd and accept its verdict. While this brief consultation was taking place, the Thracian threw himself to the ground (*decumbere*), sat back on one heel and bowed towards the earth. He no longer had the right to touch his arms; if (like that *retiarius* mentioned by Suetonius, who in mass combat recovered his trident and after raising his thumb massacred his adversaries) he violated this law by the slightest gesture he would draw upon himself the curses of the spectators.

However, the spectators were not of one mind; some raised their hands and asked for mercy, others with downward-pointing thumb (*pollice verso*) demanded the execution of the vanquished. Generally speaking, the verdict was not the product of arbitrary cruelty; it was dictated by a very rough sort of justice, a sort of 'sporting' equity, if you like. Had the gladiator shown himself cowardly, or had he let the combat drag on ignobly, the crowd, deprived of its pleasure, would assuredly have demanded his condemnation. But if he had fought well for a long time or shown exceptionally fine swordsmanship, or if luck had played a great part in his defeat, the loser had a good chance of being 'sent back'.

Perhaps the Thracian had been wrong to arouse hope of a longer and more violent combat by his haughty denial. In doubtful cases the slightest circumstance could tip the scales to one side or the other. In the first combats of an afternoon the crowd was avid for blood and was harsher than it was later on. With a final gesture the *editor*, noting that the cries for condemnation prevailed, turned down his thumb and shouted to the *hoplomachus*: '*Jugula!*' ('Cut his throat'!). From that moment a sort of collaboration was established between the movements of the two gladiators, like that which takes place in the fulfilment of a rite. As the victor, who had just put aside his shield, advanced sword in hand, the Thracian, who all this time had remained absolutely passive, half drew himself up, put one knee to the ground and gripped his executioner's thigh, just above the knee, to steady himself; the other, drawing back his free arm, placed his hand on his victim's helmet so as to hold his head firmly, and plunged his sword just below the vizor into his unprotected neck.

Gladiators, indeed, learned how to die even as they learned how to fight. Nothing counted so much in the eyes of the public as the ability to show oneself master of the slightest movement when face to face with death; that a gladiator should not have it was a disgrace, not only to himself but to the whole community, which resented it as an affront and a degradation. 'We hate those weak and suppliant gladiators', said Cicero, 'who, hands outstretched, beseech us to let them live.' Courage alone was not enough. As Cicero and Seneca have been at pains to point out, the gladiator, in order to win renown, must know above all else how to avoid the reflex which comes at the last moment; he must not try to ward off the sword or shrink away, contract his neck or try to draw back his head. He must know how to make his muscles obey the simple principles which the *lanista*, without humour, repeated on the training ground: to offer his throat to his adversary, should the need arise, to direct against it, the point of the sword, and to receive the blow, as Cicero says, 'with his whole body'. The gladiators died without removing their helmets; to take them off would have been to show another face, to falsify the games and, so far as the public was concerned, to break a complicity which was doubtless the indispensable spice to the emotions felt during the spectacle.

After the *coup de grâce* the loser fell back; he supported himself on his outstretched arm, his hand spread out, the other hand clamped to his right thigh. He remained half-seated on his defeated arms. His chest thrust out, and leaning to the right, his head drooping, he died in the position of a traveller seated on the grass, prevented from rising by great weariness.

Scarcely had the corpse been taken away than two Thracians ceremonially came forward in the manner already described. Their armour, with the exception of the helmet which was without vizor and had a very broad rim, recalled in every detail that of the recent combatant. They slashed at each other. But the shattering clash of swords striking at random on their shields could not for long conceal from the public the care each of them took to spare himself while sparing his adversary. As a crowning mediocrity, one of them, seized by some whim or driven by the hope of ending the combat rapidly without running unnecessary risks, tried to strike his adversary on the head. This way of fighting was against the rules.

The defensive armour of the gladiators was in fact worked out in accordance with a very definite principle: the protection of the places where even a very light wound could seriously handicap the fighter by preventing him from making use of all the resources of his technique. Such was the purpose of those pieces of metal and leather which covered the arms and legs, especially the joints. It was also designed to protect the head, where the least blow could be fatal even if no real combat had taken place, so that the chest alone was exposed, and it was this part of the body, hidden by the shield, which any gladiator worthy of the name had to try to reach. There was no question of maiming or brutally assassinating an adversary, only of winning a contest.

The public, by its protests, forced the Thracians to abandon such dishonest conduct and the struggle continued, as mediocre as before. Already insults were crackling along the tiers: 'They're fighting like novices!' 'A couple of chickens!' 'The criminals thrown to the beasts have more guts!' 'One could knock them down by breathing on them!' 'He's knock-kneed!' Faced with this persistent sparring, scorn soon turned to anger and the crowd, in Seneca's phrase, 'from spectators became adversaries'. Deprived of their pleasure and stamping with rage like children, the sovereign people, thinking that they were being insulted by being regaled with such a display of cowardice, loudly demanded the punishment usual in such cases. Then the *lanista* intervened. He was the proprietor of the troupe of gladiators hired for that day by the *editor*. He gave some orders and the employees appointed for this purpose, whip in hand or brandishing red-hot irons, leapt upon the Thracians, while the crowd urged them to strike, to brand the naked flesh (a practice reserved, in fact, for criminals and quite exceptional for gladiators). However, men exhausted by fear rather than fatigue, cannot be spurred on in this way. After half-heartedly starting to fight again, one of the Thracians threw away his arms and ran at top speed. The other caught him and tried to cut his throat without even waiting for a sign from the spectators. Once again the *lanista* intervened to stop an act that was contrary to propriety and tradition.

The crowd had no intention of sparing the suppliant, but such shameful precipitancy roused its indignation and it regretted that it was not able to condemn the 'victor' also. It might have been a colleague of the loser who, laconic or spitefully exact, scribbled on the walls of the barracks an inscription commemorating the event, similar to some found at Pompeii: 'Polycarpus fled', 'Officiosus fled on November 6th in the consulate of Drusus Caesar and M. Junius Norbanus.' The hysteria even overwhelmed the Vestals. One of them counted the blows, leaping up frenziedly every time the sword penetrated the flesh of the dying Thracian.

Removal of the dead

After the frantic shouts of the crowd with down-turned thumbs came a confused murmur of comments, broken by a few yells or outbursts of unsuitable joy from those who had backed the victor. After the tense expectation, the expansive gestures and the confused agitation which accompanied the prolonged tension of the spectacle, tongues were loosed and feet tapped on the worn stone. Stiffened bodies became once more aware of themselves; this was the moment to call to order the nuisance who in his enthusiasm had continually pressed his knee deeper and deeper, during the combat, into his neighbour's unprotected back, or to remove the importunate arm or shoulder of a too familiar neighbour.

The intervals, however, had long since ceased to provide the opportunities for amorous intrigue common at the Circus. It will be recalled that women had originally not been admitted to the gladiatorial shows. Later, when this prohibition, like the sumptuary laws which great ladies no longer observed, fell into disuse, no regulation had been passed to codify a practice henceforth taken for granted. In the words of Suetonius, 'confusion and the most unbridled permissiveness' became the order of the day. But Augustus, whose liking for order is well known, introduced it there, as elsewhere. By a series of decrees he separated the soldiers from the common people, assigned special seats to the married plebeians, as well as to young men clothed in the *praetextata*, their tutors and instructors being grouped in confraternities occupying the neighbouring sector. Above all, with the exception of the wives of dignitaries authorized to share the seats of the Vestals, he relegated women, who till then had attended the combats with the men, to the highest tiers, those of the third *maenianum* which overhung the terrace. It was a well-ordered crowd which stamped and challenged.

The crowd had already forgotten the corpse which lay in the middle of the arena. Some of the gladiators were resting on the sand soiled by their blood, as if sleeping after a night of passion. In the paintings that have come down to us we see them relaxed, legs wide apart, with heads thrown back and arms flung far from the chest as if they were seeking to breathe as easily as possible. A limp hand still holds in its hollow the pommel of a sword; and the mass of chest muscles, tensed by deep breathing, dominates the profile which emerges from a dense beard and thick hair.

Others, on the other hand, seem to be trying to bend their bodies into a perfect curve, or crescent. One leg is stretched forward, with raised foot. The other is withdrawn towards the belly, the foot wedged under the opposite thigh. The head rests gently on a bent elbow and there is something childlike in the manner in which the left hand, closed but not clenched, has fallen a few inches below the face, scarcely touching the ground In contradistinction the corpse, lying on its back at full length, shows something akin to a brutal rupture: beneath the swollen chest the head suddenly breaks away from the axis of the body to follow the arm which, thrown back violently, is still caught in the strap of the shield thrown to the ground. But no trace of that repugnant abandon can be seen in the others, and this perhaps is not the only instance of artistic sublimation. There is, congealed in their muscles, a little of that dignity and nobility with which the *lanista* at the training-school taught them to offer their throats when vanquished.

As the victor disappeared, laden with rewards, a personage who seemed as if he had been removed from the wall of an Etruscan tomb entered the arena; he was clothed in a close-fitting tunic and wore long boots of supple leather. His face was not altogether human. He had a nose like the beak of a bird of prey and held a long-handled mallet in his hand. He was the Etruscan Charon, preceded by a Hermes Psycopomp, brandishing a red-hot caduceus which he applied to the flesh of the vanquished man to make sure that he was really dead and not merely unconscious or wounded. Then, this proof established, Charon took possession of the dead by striking him with his mallet. As soon as Hades, according to the most archaic rites, had been assured of its prey, the *libitinarii* bore the corpse away.

They carried it off on a stretcher; sometimes a horse towed it away at the end of a long hook, leaving a furrow in the sand that was at once made good, towards the Porta Libitinaria, situated on the main axis of the amphitheatre opposite the one through which the gladiators entered. It was so called after the goddess Libitina, who presided at funerals and pleased no one. Meanwhile a second team of slaves had appeared. Some laid the dust with water, while others turned over the sand where blood had flowed, removing all traces of the preceding combat. Soon the arena was as clean as if nothing had happened.

The spectators were revived with perfumed water, with which the whole enclosure was sprayed, and which was even supplied to the upper tiers through a system of pipes. The air was stuffy and saturated with dust because of the precautions taken to protect the spectators from the rays of the sun: a sort of awning, known as the *velarium* or *velum*, formed by triangular bands fixed on masts covered the exposed part of the tiers. As the sun moved, these were moved by a system of pulleys, manned by sailors posted on top of the building. The freshness of the fine droplets loosened throats and once more the trumpets sounded, soon followed by the strains of the orchestra which accompanied the combats.

Refinements of cruelty

The next combat differed entirely from the one which had preceded it. It was a series of brief confrontations, between which there were long episodes of flight, when the music of the orchestra, in the sudden silences which fell on the arena, was charged with a special significance. The spectators did not boo when one of the men, pursued by his adversary, began to run across the arena, his face uncovered and his feet bare, balancing at arm's length a trident like that of the god Neptune, for there was nothing shameful about this flight. This was the *retiarius'* defensive weapon, indeed almost the only one; he wore no helmet and carried no shield. Nor did he wear the greaves common among the gladiators. The *retiarius* was so destitute of armour that he was sometimes made to fight on a sort of dais connected to the ground by two planks steeply inclined, so as to give him a position of advantage over his adversary. But by this he lost the advantage of mobility which compensated him for his lack of armour, and more often the combat took place on the level ground.

Thus, apart from retreat, his sole means of defence was attack; as soon as he had gained enough ground to turn without danger, he was once more on the attack, his body twisted slightly to the left by the trident which he thrust out before him, head down, to keep his adversary at a distance. In his right hand he balanced a net, which he swung round in a circular movement. But as soon as he had thrown it, his adversary ducked, raising the shield which he held in his left hand to the level of his eyes, thus checking the impetus of the meshes which were intended to envelop him. This was a fairly long rectangular shield, for the other combatant was a *secutor* (so called because he 'pursued' his antagonist) and not the *myrmillo* or the semi-legendary Gaul whose helmet, surmounted by a fish similar to that which sometimes decorated the shoulder-piece of the *retiarius*, underlined the symbolic nature of the struggle.

Meanwhile, the *secutor*, as soon as the dry rattle of the meshes against the metal had warned him that he was safe, counter-attacked, sword in hand; but now the *retiarius* had no time to recover his net before running away. It was a first step towards defeat for, well thrown, this weapon could by itself decide the issue of the combat. In fact, the little cord which bordered it and was used to recover it in the case of failure, also enabled him to imprison his adversary completely and, if not to throw him to the ground, at least to throw him seriously off balance at a moment when his safety depended on the speed of his reactions; even if the net remained free and floated on his shoulders, he could not resist the assault of the *retiarius* unless he had had the luck to keep his sword-arm free.

The loss of his net forced the *retiarius* to change his tactics; he seized the trident in both hands, the left hand near the prongs and the right gripping the end of the shaft. Thus stationed, he at first kept the *secutor* at bay by the full length of his weapon, then attacked, thrusting the trident violently downward as if to pin a monster to the ground, or raising it above the shield to hook the vizored helmet which, perfectly smooth and without any ornament, offered very little chance of a hold. The *secutor* parried the blows with his sword rather than by using his shield. Perhaps he was afraid that blows of such violence would make the prongs of the trident slip dangerously on its surface. But it was also evident that he was trying to make it fall from the hands of the *retiarius* and, with this in view, went so far as to use his shield as an offensive weapon; seizing the moment of an attack from below, he thrust it down on the inclined shaft, throwing his whole weight upon it, to make his adversary lose his grip. The latter, forced to draw aside to avoid the sword threatening his flank, while all the time resisting this terrible pressure, had great difficulty in breaking away. In fact, the exchanges more and more became trials of brute force, iron against iron, where the nature of his weapons did not favour the *retiarius*.

He changed tactics once more; he disengaged the dagger which he was holding with his left hand against the shaft of the trident and transferred it to his right hand; but no longer having the whole length of the staff before him to keep his adversary at a distance, he found increasing difficulty in avoiding close fighting. Parrying one of his adversary's blows on the left, he caught the *secutor's* shield on the right and he succeeded in tearing it away; but, thrown off balance by the effort, the two men rolled on the ground and the trident flew several yards away. They did not think of recovering their arms but threw themselves on each other, crawling over the sand in a sort of duel with knives. At each movement the spectators, now registering the fight mechanically, shouted in the ears of imaginary neighbours and informed the amphitheatre of what each wished to see: 'He's going to strike!', 'He's missed!'. No one thought of claiming the *missio*, even though both gladiators were undoubtedly wounded; death must ensue or one must raise his hand. Suddenly the *secutor* fell full length.

The *retiarius*, instead of dealing a mortal blow, might perhaps have been satisfied by paralyzing his opponent with a severe wound, thus leaving him the chance of being 'sent back'. Even now, when carried away by the frenzy of the combat, the spectators, for all that they tended to be caught up by the impetus of the victor and to turn down their thumbs, might perhaps have been impressed by the courage of the *secutor*. But among gladiators there was an old maxim engraved on the walls of their barracks: *Ut quis quem vicerit occidat.* (Kill the vanquished whoever he may be.) It was a warning given from beyond the tomb by those unfortunates who, having one day spared an adversary, received death at his hand, some years later, at another meeting.

The victor then received the palm of victory which he waved towards the spectators as he walked round the arena, and afterwards a sum of money or some precious objects. Under the Emperor Claudius this scene was invested with a touch of originality; Claudius liked to count out, one by one, the golden pieces which he handed over to the victor, in the manner of a shopkeeper, instead of handing them to him all at once, and the people greatly appreciated such good-humoured generosity. But the *retiarius* was in no way freed from the servitude of his profession; he was obliged to appear once more in the arena unless his engagement was coming to an end or unless the emperor, to reward his merit, asked for his premature liberation. He was then give the *rudis*, a wooden wand, at once tool and symbol. It was used in fact as a side-arm in simulated combats and sometimes during training; it was also the insignia which the *doctor* or the *lanista* held in his hand as a mark of authority when, acting as umpire or referee, he threw himself between the combatants to separate them if one had committed an irregularity. Thus it was given ceremonially to the victorious gladiator at his last combat as a sign of mastery and manumission.

In the long run these spectacles, the rhythm and technique of which never varied, became for that very reason monotonous. So there soon appeared gladiators who attracted attention by some unusual feature of equipment or method. First of all, there were the *essedarii*, who fought from chariots which turned and twisted or halted suddenly to the flourishes of a hydraulic organ. Here the combatant was no longer the sole arbiter of his own life; it depended on the skill or clumsiness of the slave who held the reins. Then there were the *equites*, or cavaliers, richly caparisoned, protected by a cuirass, thigh-pieces and a round shield, who fought with a lance, the *dimachaeri* who fought without a shield but with a sword in either hand, or the *laquearii* whose offensive weapon was a kind of lassoo and who, like the *retiarii*, were exposed almost without defence to the sword-blows of their adversaries.

But in this composite gallery where, as if in a museum of antiquities, all the weapons and techniques of the peoples formerly conquered by Rome were to be found, the *andabates* were by far the most picturesque protagonists. They confronted each other gropingly, their heads imprisoned in full-vizored helmets, and, in Dezobry's phrase, looked like 'machines launched into the arena to be abandoned there'. Luck, however, played little

59

part in the outcome of the combat; a coat of mail covered the whole body, so that the blows which a gladiator beating the air with his sword chanced to land were harmless instead of mortal. In order to deceive his adversary, the *andabate* might well manoeuvre in the arena with all the precautions of a skin-diver in deep water anxious not to scare the fish; but it was not trickery any more than luck, but skill in swordsmanship and strength which were finally the decisive factors of victory, since the sole method of winning was to strike at the joints of the cuirass. The training which they received at the barracks turned them not merely into good gladiators but also into good players of blind man's buff.

There were also other spices to whet the appetite of the crowd. Certainly there could not be produced in the Colosseum those armies which the emperors, elsewhere, sometimes commanded to engage each other in a real carnage. But small troupes of gladiators, all similarly armed, were brought into the arena. They fought in regular formation—some kneeling, sword in hand, ready to spring up, at the feet of their comrades who awaited upright the enemy's assault—against an equal number of combatants with different weapons. Or sometimes the gladiator who had just conquered was not permitted to leave the arena, but was immediately made to confront a second adversary, fresh and in good trim, who had been held in reserve and was called *tertiarius* or *suppositicius*.

Another of these refinements consisted of a special form of combat which Augustus had formerly prohibited because of its excessive cruelty, but which had none the less survived him— the combat *sine missione*. In normal conditions, the two gladiators fairly often left the arena alive, either because the loser had earned his pardon or because, after a long and desperate struggle, neither of the two had been able to gain an advantage over the other, something common enough as is proved, for example, by the trophies of the gladiator Flamma; they were then *stantes missi*, that is to say sent back while still standing and fighting and both received the palm of victory. In the *munera sine missione*, on the other hand, no quarter was ever given. There had always to be a corpse on the sand and the repetition of these murders throughout an afternoon turned the *munus* into a real carnage.

Finally, when the spectacle had been too second-rate, the shouting public demanded that famous gladiators who had shown their worth, and who were often re-engaged after having been liberated, should appear in the arena. To produce such champions cost the emperor a small fortune, but he could not refuse without seriously displeasing the spectators. It was therefore a combat which displayed all the resources of sword-play that brought the afternoon spectacle to an end. This, it is true, was so only for reasonable and sensible men, for while in the lower hall known as the *spoliarium*, situated close to the Porta Libitinaria, the *confectores* killed the vanquished gladiators whom the swords of their adversaries had not struck to death and took from the line of corpses the armour from which the sand of the arena still fell, on the tiers the crowd struggled, each man trying to snatch for himself the tallies projected at full speed by a machine called *linea*, or goods in kind thrown pell-mell by the attendants.

The struggle was a fierce one. Wounds and fractures were by no means rare in these pitched battles in which real 'professionals' took part. These were plebeians who had borrowed money against a pledge of the booty which they expected to gain when the public largesse was distributed, or those who, for a fixed sum, pledged themselves to hand over to a speculator everything they could lay their hands on. This was enough to explain why honest men preferred to leave the amphitheatre before the *sparsio* began.

It was indeed a tradition that the games should be accompanied by bounties to the people. Sometimes they took the form of banquets uniting at a single table senators, knights and humble citizens. More often they took the form of a *sparsio*, that is to say a distribution which was a lottery in a double sense, both because of the method of distribution described above and also because the tallies which rained down on the tiers represented, as in burlesque lotteries in which a man could win ten flies or ten

61

elephants, lots of very unequal value, from a couple of chickens to a ship or a country house, to say nothing of a tame bear.

The ultimate pleasure was the emperor's; he could, standing in his box, watch for a few moments the spectacle of the Roman people scrimmaging among the tiers at his feet in hope of a tessera decorated with the sails of a ship, or a half-melon bearing the figure 3—one of the forms of the ancient treble chance.

A parody of a duel

In the streets of Rome, at sunrise, one came across, besides pedestrians, only sedan-chairs, litters and a few horsemen. Because of the narrowness of the streets and the numerous accidents caused by chariots driven at full speed by scatter-brained snobs, traffic was strictly controlled by the Lex Julia Municipalis. Private chariots (*curri*) and carts used for the transport of goods (*plaustra*) were forbidden in daytime up to the third century AD. There were, however, certain exceptions in favour of vehicles destined for the transport of materials of public utility, for example those coming from the demolition of old buildings or necessary for the construction of new ones.

According to the letter of the law, those which, on the stroke of the first hour, made their way towards the Statilius Taurus amphitheatre belonged, so to speak, to this category, for they were transporting prisoners taken from the state prisons. Nothing distinguished them, however, from the heavy vehicles of the carters except their wheels which, instead of being solid, had spokes. Behind each vehicle marched two guards and the length of the convoy gave it a ritual aspect. The leading carts bore freeborn men condemned to death for civil-law crimes—murder or armed theft—some of whom, sentenced in the provinces, had been sent to Rome and placed at the disposal of the *editor*. In the others was a strange medley of barbarian prisoners, deserters, freed men and slaves. This last class was by far the most numerous. Apart from those whom misery had driven to join the bands of brigands always plentiful in Italy, there was a whole procession of unfortunates, now *sine domino*, with no other master save death. From the earliest days of the Empire, many laws had unquestionably been passed giving slaves guarantees which at one time they had not enjoyed, being wholly in the power of their masters. But no one could now condemn his slaves to fight wild beasts without the consent of a magistrate who judged of the appropriateness of this punishment. Above all, slaves had the generally exercisable right to bring complaints against their masters before the town prefect.

Nothing could be farther from the truth than to generalize from some exceptional cases and picture their condition as unrelievedly wretched. It varied according to their own skill and the shortcomings of their masters. Yet if one can believe what one reads, abuses, even though rare, existed none the less sometimes going as far as the most unjustified cruelties. What legal recourse could prevail against the standing of a master in favour at court or the silver of a rich banker? Thus of the men found here, their hands tied behind their backs or bound together by a rope round their necks, some had done nothing to deserve their fate, as for example the tutor of Glycon mentioned in the *Satyricon* who had been surprised while pleasuring his patroness. But anyone who knows the degree of corruption in Roman society of that time—when many husbands merely played the part of a convenient screen—may well hesitate to declare a man of servile origin responsible in such circumstances. Petronius indeed was indignant. 'Is it the slave's fault that he is forced to act thus? It is rather that old shitbag who deserves to be tossed on the bull's horns.' There was also the band of fugitive slaves captured by the soldiers, men such as Androcles, who preferred to live for three years on raw meat in the desert rather than submit to the harassments and cruelties of his master, the proconsul.

To reach the amphitheatre one had to cross almost the entire city. When they reached the Campus Martius, where the murmur of the crowd massed on the tiers could already be heard, a sleeping prisoner suddenly twisted on his bench; pretending to let his head fall, he thrust it between the spokes of the wheel and lay blood-stained, his neck twisted and eyes protruding. Like Cato, 'this man of base stock by a magnificent effort had reached a place of safety'.

On another day a 'barbarian', a German, went to the latrines—it was the only way of escaping being under guard for a few seconds—and choked himself by plunging down his throat the piece of wood tipped with a sponge that was used for the vilest purposes. There is also the incident of the twenty-nine Saxon pirates fallen into the hands of the soldiers, who strangled one another in prison with their bare hands. One could cite many other cases of less spectacular suicides by condemned men who had not the luck to die simply by having their heads cut off by the executioner outside the city walls, but whom the amphitheatre awaited one fine morning.

It was on the stroke of the seventh hour that Seneca, on one such day, happened to pass the amphitheatre and was drawn by one of those sudden caprices, which his sophistical philosophy was powerless to repress immediately, to enter the arena. The programme, doubtless, quickly lulled his already uneasy conscience; he knew that at that hour of the day he would not have to endure the repugnant spectacle of the blood-stained sand. He was expecting farcical interludes.

It was midday. The tiers were emptying. The Romans were leaving the amphitheatre to snatch a bite and to relax after the tensions of the spectacle. This was, to tell the truth, a fairly recent custom, dating from the first half of the century. Before that, it seems to have been the custom to attend the games all day long, without stopping for a meal; but under the Empire only a few spectators remained on the tiers. Other than a few fanatics, these were mostly plebeians who were sitting in free seats. To obtain them, they had risen in the middle of the night and queued until dawn. They had had to elbow and jostle to keep their places in the crush, happy not to have been driven away with blows because the noise of their chatter disturbed the sleep of the emperor's favourite horse. There was, therefore, no question of abandoning for a meagre lunch a place won by such effort and

7. The *retiarius*, who has lost his trident, raises his finger to ask for mercy. The winning *secutor* is left-handed, a peculiarity always dreaded in a combat. Colchester Museum. (Photo Boudot-Lamotte)

8. A *secutor*. Small bronze from the Roman Museum at Avenches (Switzerland). (Photo Bersier)

which they were sure not to find empty again in the afternoon for the second part of the performance.

During the interval some entertainment had to be found to amuse this crowd which could scarcely be said to represent the cream of Roman society. This usually took the form of farcical interludes or displays of sword-play, more or less parodies, in which the best-known players were the *paegniarii*. Their bodies were almost completely covered by fairly wide bandages which formed a garment; a shield, attached by straps to the left arm, ended in a sort of crook. One raised a staff in his right hand and another let a very long whip drag along the ground. They are shown thus on a mosaic, in attitudes not unlike those of our hockey players. We do not know what were the ups and downs of the combat or how exactly it came to an end, but it was not pursued to the death. So far as we can see, it was a question of knockabout weapons, and the combats were more like crude floggings than gladiatorial encounters.

On this day, however, there was nothing of the sort. The massacre had begun. Modern civilization surrounds the execution of criminals with a screen of secrecy; high prison walls, veils, an early morning or nocturnal hour, all have their part in concealing the act from the world of the living. This guilt-laden shame did not exist at Rome. It often happened that criminals condemned to death were sent *en masse* to the arena instead of being executed. They were then *noxii ad gladium ludi damnati*, condemned to the sword in the amphitheatre.

These privileged ones—for only criminals of free condition had the right to this noble weapon, slaves and freedmen being reserved for a more ignoble punishment—were driven two by two before the crowd. There was no question of a real combat, and these men, who had had no sort of training, had nothing in common with the professional gladiators. The first man was armed with a dagger. Another was then driven into the arena half-naked, completely unarmed, without even a shield. He had no chance. He fled. The indignant shouts of the crowd immediately drew from the enclosure servants armed with whips and branding

E

irons always kept there in order to drive on those wanting courage for the 'combat'. The same thing happened when the second of the pair hesitated to use his dagger, either from aversion or by design, in order to postpone for a few moments the hour of his own death. For, as soon as he had killed his opponent, he himself was disarmed and had to expose his defenceless torso to the blows of a newcomer. There was no end save death and the massacre continued without respite until only a single criminal remained. His throat was then cut, or he was sent back to appear at the next performance.

Such, at least, is the generally accepted version. There can be no question of any of the criminals escaping. In other respects, however, it does not tally with the very precise details given by Seneca in a letter to Lucilius in which he describes these killings. It is astonishing, first of all, that on comparing these combats with those of the professional gladiators and asserting that the crowd preferred the first to the second he contents himself with saying that the reason for this preference was the absence of defensive armour and technical refinement. He stresses these two points without making a single allusion to the fact that one of the combatants was completely unarmed—a fact, moreover, which he never mentions or leaves to be understood. And this is far from being the only improbability.

Before touching on moral considerations we must listen in to one of these combats as far as we can through the shouts of the crowd. One of the combatants, seized with panic, has taken to his heels. Here is Seneca's report: 'Kill him! Lash him! Burn him! Why does he meet the sword in such a cowardly way? Why does he strike so feebly? Why doesn't he die game? Whip him to meet his wounds! Let them receive blow for blow, with chests bare and exposed to the stroke!' It is hard to see how this could be done if one of the men only had his bare hands to confront an adversary who, with a gesture, could keep him at a distance and who would certainly kill him as soon as he tried to come to grips. It seems more reasonably to admit, as the phrase *mutuos ictos* suggests, a certain reciprocity and that the originality of these combats lay in the fact that both combatants were without means of defence.

This would have been enough to make the cruelty insupportable. In fact, among professional gladiators the chest was exposed (protected only by manipulation of the shield) while arms and legs were protected in order to avoid wounds which were not mortal but which would have diminished the interest of the combat. They were expected to display skilled swordsmanship and the crowd was indignant if they were senselessly maimed. Here, on the contrary, every blow counted. The clumsier they were the more numerous their wounds and the bloodier the combat. That was the meaning of the phrase quoted above: 'Whip him to meet his wounds'. He was no more than an open wound covered with dust and dripping with blood, and it was in such a state that he, if he had had the luck to overcome his adversary, would have to confront another one a few moments later.

The crowd, as may be imagined, was the leading actor in these bloody dramas. It was doubtless not merely for stylistic effect or to attack more rigorously the degradation which he denounced that Seneca records its reactions in such detail. None of the motives which made the ordinary gladiator risk his life existed for these men: neither honour which owing to the long apprenticeship of the training-school had acquired the nature of a conditioned reflex, nor the hope of reward, nor even that of saving their own lives in the event of victory. The whips and branding-irons were there to force them to meet their foe. But how could these men have plunged into combat if they had not been gradually carried away by the excitement which swept the tiers, egged on by the exhortations, the shouts, the encouragements, to such an extent as altogether to forget the meaninglessness of their struggle—and to follow instinct alone?

'In the morning,' says Seneca, 'they throw men to the lions and bears; at noon, they throw them to the spectators.'

It is clear beyond doubt that criminals had their throats cut in the arena. But it is quite pointless to blacken the picture by generalizing from a procedure which remained exceptional.

67

We must in any case clearly distinguish the midday combats not only from the ordinary *munera* but even more from the *munera sine missione* which have already been described. The principle was entirely different; mercy was never accorded to the loser, whatever courage he might have shown, and only one man would emerge living from the struggle. The gladiator could not, as in the usual combats, count upon the clemency of the spectators. It was victory or death. Here, it was a question of a special form of mass execution, carefully organized, in which the criminal lost the one thing that still remained to him—the possibility of dying with dignity in relative solitude.

A bastard spectacle: the naumachias

In the naumachias, as at the midday games, criminals were set to fight one another, but the combats took place on water. Small troupes appeared in them, as sometimes in the *munera*, but there were real armies also; we read of 19,000 appearing in one of them.

Historians confirm that these naval battles sometimes took place in the amphitheatres where, by a system of reservoirs and channels, the arena could be flooded or drained at will. Martial pretends astonishment: 'There was land until a moment ago. Can you doubt it? Wait until the water, draining away, puts an end to the combats; it will happen right away. Then you will say: the sea was there a moment ago.'

But this method was exceptional and we very often think we recognize in provincial amphitheatres a means of flooding where only drainage channels exist. Furthermore, it was not possible to stage grandiose battles. Caesar, Augustus, Domitian, therefore had special basins dug in Rome, known as naumachias, the word serving both for the spectacles and for the places where they were staged. That of Augustus necessitated the construction of an aqueduct 22,000 paces long to bring to Rome the water needed to fill a basin which measured 598 yards by 393, specially excavated in order to stage a combat in which between 2,000 and 3,000 men took part. It served subsequently, it is true, for the watering of the gardens and furnished an additional source for the provision of water to the city. Claudius did not want to rely on any of the usual solutions; he gave a naumachia on the Fucino lake which, taking up once more a project earlier conceived by Caesar, was linked to the Liris river by a series of imposing construction works.

This sort of spectacle, which first appeared in the times of Caesar, exuberantly displayed the youth of an empire rich in resources. But it had a brief existence; naumachias are no longer mentioned after the first century, nor were they ever staged with the regularity of the *munera*. How could they have been, considering the enormous expenses involved? It was not merely a question of finding the monies needed to finance a complex organization, the construction and equipment of a fleet and the destruction of a vast number of human lives, for in this slave economy men also had their price; the very water intended to engulf these riches cost a fortune, for the sea was too inconvenient and the bays too far away to serve for such entertainments.

Naturally, the naumachias were no mere imitations of a battle; blood was shed in floods and it even happened that none of the combatants emerged from the mêlée alive. Sometimes, however, as after the naumachia on the Fucino lake, the survivors were granted mercy, which could only have been a respite, for a criminal, at least by law, remained a criminal. To compel these men to kill one another stringent safety measures were taken in case of need; Claudius, for example, had a circle of rafts placed all around the Fucino lake on which the praetorians, ranged in maniples, closed every way of escape.

To this pitiless realism was added a search for picturesque and exotic travesties. It was customary for the naumachia to represent some famous naval battle. Greek history above all was ransacked for examples, either because of the vogue for things Greek then current at Rome, or quite simply because it abounded in picturesque episodes. Thus one saw, under Augustus and under Nero, the Athenians twice defeat the Persians in the roads of Salamis, the Corcyreans destroy the Corinthian fleet and

69

kill all the captives, while, under Caesar the snobbery of the time forced the criminals to die on triremes flying Egyptian colours.

These fictions naturally involved recourse to a more or less complex *mise en scène*: for example, a fort was built on an island in the naumachia excavated by Augustus so that the 'Athenians', victors over the Syracusans, could take it by assault before the eyes of the spectators; on the Fucino lake a triton rose out of the waters and gave the signal for the combat to begin. The few details reported by Tacitus lead one to think that the striving for exactitude was pushed to the utmost. The combat had to follow the usual phases of a naval battle and include displays of everything that might arouse interest: the skill of the pilots, or the force of the rowers, the power of the various types of vessel, or the play of the siege-engines mounted on breastworks which had been erected at the ends of the rafts surrounding the lake.

This taste for historical pageants was not limited to the naumachias; in the last days of the Republic the ceremonies of the triumphs, at once religious and political, had already called for a spectacle intended to impress the crowd and satisfy its curiosity. The procession stretched as far as the Capitol, displaying, in addition to the often sumptuous spoils taken from the enemy, tableaux depicting the most picturesque episodes of the campaign of which the general was celebrating the victorious outcome. Claudius went even further in the same vein; he caused the capture and sack of a city and the submission of the kings of Britain to be staged 'according to nature' in Rome itself. It might be said that this was the manner in which a people, unsure of its imaginative powers, showed its taste for historical romance, were it not that a detail gave it another and more special significance; Claudius presided at this spectacle not in the usual fashion but in that of a man in charge of the capture or surrender of a city or the submission of a king—wearing a general's cloak. This nonsense of a prince 'triumphing', if one may so call it, at a theatrical performance cannot be attributed entirely to mental derangement. We shall soon have occasion to speak once more of this tendency to play with reality which became one of the characteristic aspects of the spectacles under the Empire.

Shorn of these complications, the naumachia was, basically, a sort of 'super-production' where the taste for death on the grand scale was allied to that of pure spectacle. The Romans demanded something more to add spice to the shedding of blood; in the gladiatorial combats it was the art of swordsmanship, the 'suspense' of a struggle whose issue was long in doubt. Here it was the stage setting and the story. But it was rare that this latter element prevailed in the naumachias; only one case is on record in which, after the flooding of the amphitheatre, a display of fishes and 'marine monsters' was deemed sufficient. The attraction of the water, strong as it may have been for this people which took long to become accustomed to the sea, was never able to make it forget the taste for blood, of which every known form of the naumachia shows traces, whether it was the refinement which consisted of erecting wooden bridges over the water on which gladiators had to fight, or in the transformation of a part of the Circus Flaminius into a basin in which, on one day, about thirty crocodiles were slaughtered.

The only pleasure which escaped this contamination and formed a specific element in this type of spectacle was perhaps that which the Romans obtained from the quick changes of scene possible in the amphitheatre. It frequently happened that a few minutes after the staging of a naval battle, gladiators appeared on the drained soil. Thus Nero, in the course of a single day, staged a 'hunt' in the arena, then flooded the amphitheatre for a naumachia, drained it again for gladiatorial combats, and then flooded it once more to give the populace a banquet on board ship. It is hard not to see in this taste for the artificial the rudimentary elements of the baroque, manifest in the invention of the silver triton which an ingenious mechanism caused to rise in the centre of the lake to give the signal for the battle.

The difficulty of interpreting the monuments

We have seen that the interest of the gladiatorial combats lay

71

partly in the fact that, generally speaking, two men faced each other in the arena, that their methods of fighting and their arms were quite different, without, however, giving either an advantage over the other. One could even speak of a sort of law of balance or complementation; if a gladiator, like the *retiarius*, was provided with three offensive weapons, he was in return deprived of all means of covering himself; if, like the *hoplomachus*, he had an abnormally large shield, he had to make use of it to protect not only his vital parts but also his limbs, where a wound could restrict his freedom of movement. By uncovering himself, he took more risks than his adversary, the Thracian, whose arms and legs were protected by leather or even metal. And if a gladiator, as was perhaps the case with the *myrmillo*, fought with bare body, without being compensated for this disadvantage by the size of his shield, we may be sure that he employed a particularly dangerous fighting technique or offensive weapon.

The existence of pairs *ne varietur*, fixed in relation to specific affinities, explains the other characteristic we have tried to elucidate. The combat consisted of a series of 'figures', involving well-determined phases, and its evolution obeyed typical forms whose number was limited. The *retiarius*, for example, could win straight away by casting his net; or, if this manoeuvre failed, by wielding his trident, which resulted in far more vigorous confrontations. If he succeeded in tearing away his opponent's shield, the contest was almost won, but if, on the contrary, he let his trident be snatched away from him, as must often have happened since he was provided with a dagger as an auxiliary weapon, he had to have exceptional skill to defeat in hand to hand combat an adversary who by comparison, was now armed to the teeth.

The ups and downs of the struggle, its brutal turns of fortune, the progression by which death could be seen approaching nearer and nearer to a man each time he lost one of his weapons, turned these combats into an art for the connoisseur. In every situation a good or bad reaction was possible. A good one could enable a combatant to extricate himself from a desperate situation;

clumsiness at a critical moment was equivalent to a death sentence. The spectators knew all the parries, all the ruses, and sometimes, from the height of the tiers, put a man on guard against his adversary's manoeuvres, shouting instructions to him.

The prime importance of sword-play and its rules explains among other things why the public showed its anger against gladiators when they seemed hesitant; the combat then became a shapeless duel lacking all the interest given it by technique. These refinements, however, did not preclude a certain monotony. There were, certainly, some variants which might be called titbits. It could happen, for instance, that the *secutor*, entangled in the *retiarius'* net, managed to free himself. But the number of these, like that of the regular figures, was limited and, generally speaking, when one had seen a few combats one had seen thousands. Thus, by varying the weapons of the gladiators or by matching them in unfamiliar ways, attempts were sometimes made to whet the curiosity of the public.

The organization of the combats was therefore based on the existence of differing classes or types of arms (*armaturae*) opposed to one another according to more or less fixed rules. The *retiarius* never fought another *retiarius*, but always a *secutor* or, more rarely, a *myrmillo*. This last, at least at a certain period, was the habitual adversary of the Thracian etc.

We know fifteen of these categories, whose existence is proved both by written accounts and by inscriptions. Nothing, however, proves that our list is complete. Certain monuments provide us with portraits of combatants who, by their dress or their arms, correspond to none of the categories we know—for example, the hitherto unknown one discovered by Robert after comparison of two bas-reliefs, whose specialty was to fight the *retiarius*. This man used a weapon that was both offensive and defensive, a sort of cone which protected the left forearm, at the end of which there was fixed a rod ending in a crescent which presumably allowed him to hook or pull away the *retiarius'* net. Thus, once the *retiarius* had cast his net and failed to recover it, the other gladiator abandoned this cumbrous and now useless cone in order to fight with his sword alone; this original weapon, which he held in his left hand, naturally deprived him of a shield but, according to the principle stated above, he was protected against the jabs of the trident by a coat of mail which covered his whole body, including his right arm.

These gaps are, however, of small importance in comparison with those which exist in our records concerning the more usual classes of gladiators. In some cases we have great difficulty in saying exactly how one class differed from another, and sometimes we find it impossible to describe their arms with any accuracy despite the large number of monuments which the Roman passion for this type of spectacle has bequeathed to us. Their interpretation often poses insoluble problems.

For example, despite the fact that the *retiarius* is of all types of gladiators the one about whom there is scarcely anything mysterious, because his strange weapons make him easy to identify, only one of the many examples of *retiarii* known to us is clearly provided with a net. From this one might perhaps be tempted to conclude that the use of this weapon was unusual. However, it is just this that has given the *retiarius* his name; and when Juvenal speaks of this gladiator, he characterizes him by two images which are many times repeated: he is the man with the cloak who runs across the arena, but he is also the combatant whose enigmatic hand balances the net.

In fact, there are many explanations for its absence on the monuments; artists frequently omitted the sword and shield, the position of which the gladiator's stance made sufficiently clear. They had even more reason not to depict an object even harder to represent when it formed no part of the background. One can also assume that in a picture of a combat the net with which the *retiarius* was originally provided is no longer in his possession because he has already thrown it without success and has been unable to recover it. Finally, it is certain that some of these gladiators really lacked this weapon.

Furthermore, within each of these categories weapons and armour were subject to numerous variations. These are partly explained by the fact that weapons and fighting techniques were not immutable over so long a time in any category; some probably evolved until they became completely transformed. There is also no doubt but that local custom, here and there, impressed a particular character on this or that type of weapon. In Gaul, for example, in the Rhône valley, certain curious variants, out of step with the usages of Rome, have been noted. The type of weapon depicted in the second and third centuries had not been known in the capital since the first century, as Georges Ville has pointed out in his monograph on the Zliten mosaic written for the International Congress on Mosaic in 1963. But one may ask whether these variants did not in certain cases have a more precise significance, indicative of the specialized adaptation of standard weapons unknown to us as seems to be suggested by a passage from Suetonius: the reference is to the *retiarii tunicati*. As the context in no way requires a qualifying adjective, one must conclude that he is referring to a particular type of *retiarius*.

The vast number of such details is a source of insoluble contradictions. Faced with a dumb monument, we are far from sure that we are looking at this or that specific type of gladiator except when the texts provide us with sufficiently accurate details of his weapon or costume. But this is rarely so; we possess no text which treats of gladiators as a whole. The ones from which we get our information are essentially allusive. Seneca, who sometimes uses a wealth of detail, compares the sage to the gladiator, Cicero and Quintilian the orator. Thus we are better informed about his handling of the sword itself than about the nature of his weapons. As to establishing the specific nature of each, we can only make a guess. To tell the truth, the specialists who have studied the question over the last century have not refrained from making such guesses; in particular, they have abused a procedure which consists in giving the names Samnite, *hoplomachus* or *secutor* to this or that gladiator represented on some monument in order to draw general conclusions. This has given birth to comprehensive systems as numerous as they are

75

arbitrary. It is enough merely to mention them, since none of them stands up to a more detailed examination.

Our lack of certainty here is such that even the less ambitious classifications now once more accepted are to some extent inconsistent. Such, for example, as the one based on the distinction between heavy and light gladiators, a criterion which undeniably corresponds to reality. Apart from the fact that one cannot see what role the *provocator* plays in this systematic arrangement, it also has the drawback of opposing the *secutor* to gladiators like the *hoplomachus* or the Samnite, whose arms are virtually the same. Any classification which tries to avoid this type of inconsistency must rely so heavily on guesswork that it scarcely merits the name.

Evolution of the gladiatorial art: the successors of the Samnite

Enough has already been said about the *retiarii*. It suffices to recall that they were never made to fight one another, even in troupe fighting, but always gladiators of another category, *secutores* or *myrmillones*. Enough has also been said about the Thracians whose adversaries were usually the *hoplomachi* or the *myrmillones* and who, more rarely, were made to fight each other. These were called the 'little shields' or, probably more accurately, comprised a 'faction' of gladiators called by this name, for or against whom the spectators passionately took sides.

Less well known than these two types of gladiators, easily identifiable thanks to their special armament, the group which includes the Samnite, the *secutor* and doubtless also the *hoplomachus* must be mentioned, if only because the kinship of their weapons is evident. It is that of the ordinary infantryman, sword and shield—of the type known as *scutum*, quadrangular and concave. This kinship is further explained by the fact that they were related by descent. It is noticeable that the Samnite, formerly frequently mentioned in the texts, is no longer mentioned after the first days of the Empire, a period in which, on the contrary, the *hoplomachus* and the *secutor* first appear. We must therefore conclude, in agreement with a very ancient hypothesis, that this disappearance was due to some specialization of which the precise nature has escaped us, as it has of course in the case of most of the details which differentiated these three categories. Except in special cases (where for instance the adversary is a *retiarius*) we have no sure criterion for distinguishing them.

The ancient origin of the Samnites is attested by Livy; in 310 B.C. the Campanians, in mockery and hatred of the Samnites on whom, in alliance with the Romans, they had just inflicted a bloody defeat, gave this name to the gladiators who were made to fight during their banquets, rigged out in the sumptuous arms left by the vanquished on the battlefield; these consisted of a peculiarly shaped *scutum* flaring out slightly at the top to protect the shoulders and chest and ending in a V-shape for ease of handling, a plumed helmet which gave the warrior an imposing appearance, an *ocrea* on the left leg; and finally, a sort of cuirass (*spongia*) covering the chest.

We find no trace on the monuments of this last piece of protective armour, of which Tertullian speaks elsewhere when discussing the *retiarii*, and also nothing of the tapered shield. But a type of gladiator existed, very frequently represented, whose characteristics correspond, in essentials, to this description; his plumed helmet does not allow him to be identified with certainty, for this was a peculiarity common to other gladiators; moreover there are, in any one category, such widely different variations in dress that what he is wearing does not furnish a useful criterion. A band protects the right ankle, while the left leg is protected by an *ocrea* which stops below the knee—very different from that of the Thracian which, as we have seen, covered a part of the thigh. At a certain epoch it was perhaps to the Thracians that the Samnites were opposed, since these last had not yet disappeared when the Thracians first made their appearance at the time of Sulla.

The speciality of the *secutor* was to fight the *retiarius* and he was probably confounded with the *contraretiarius* mentioned in the inscription. There are, in fact, no proofs that he could have been opposed to any other type of gladiator.

His armour is essentially the same as the Samnite's. The helmet alone has a special form; it is almost spherical. Neither arm is protected. The *secutor* is, if you like, a light gladiator; none the less, the description is only half correct. Urbicus, whose portrait has been preserved for us on a bas-relief, with a mention of the category to which he belonged, seems to all intents and purposes naked. His entirely bald skull (his helmet rests on a stake fixed in the ground) no doubt adds to this impression. There is something of the rugby player about him. He is thick-set, broad-shouldered. His eyes, which one would assume to be bright because of the fixity of his gaze, stare obstinately at something beyond his adversary. He is caught full-face as if suddenly halted in his movements, ready to resume his attack, brandishing his naked sword in one hand and his shield in the other. To look at him one can easily understand that the danger to the *retiarius* lies more in the force and shock of his adversary than in the mobility suggested by his name. Their struggle, moreover, was supposed to symbolize that of water and fire, on the one side pure movement, elusive, on the other the irresistible force of the flame. This symbolism is perhaps not so open to doubt as may be thought, since we have seen a *secutor* call himself Flamma.

For the reasons which we have mentioned, the *hoplomachus* was generally associated with this type of gladiator. Two lines of Martial—'You were an oculist and now you are a *hoplomachus*. You have not changed your profession'—have led some people to identify him with these cataphractic gladiators encased in iron, who could be reached only if they were without a breastplate, or through the holes pierced in it at eye level.

But to admit this interpretation would mean that the *hoplomachi* fought only among themselves, which does not seem to have been the case.

The enigma of the myrmillones

Here again, nothing enables us clearly to distinguish the *myrmillones* and the Gauls from the preceding categories; although fighting also with sword and shield, they were it seems without protective armour.

Of all the gladiators, the *myrmillo* is the one who has been given the most varied descriptions; at one time, the sybilline allusions of Ammianus Marcellinus led to the belief that he was a 'cataphractic' gladiator with heavy weapons, a breastplate and clad in iron; at another, Festus and etymology combined to suggest that he was merely the regular adversary of the *retiarius*. Others have asserted that he was Greek by name and Greek also in his arms and his method of fighting; he was said to carry the *scutum* and the straight sword 'reminiscent of Thessaly'. And these are not the only solutions which have been proposed. This confusion is, moreover, at once evident when one examines the monuments. For example, in the Louvre there is a little bronze of a gladiator labelled *Myrmillo;* the hooked vizor, with two shutters, closes over the face with a touch of malice which makes the tiny holes pierced at eyelevel more alarming. Crouching, and pointing his curved blade in a menacing gesture, he looks like an aggressive and obstinate insect, an enigma which can serve to show how much our idea of gladiators is coloured by romanticism and sentimentality. But he is a Thracian; the shape of his sword and of his small square shield, the greaves (*cnemides*) which he wears on each leg, prove it beyond doubt.

We have, on the other hand, a bas-relief with an inscription assuring us that it really does represent a *myrmillo*. The man is wearing only a loincloth; arms, legs and torso are completely bare. His left hand holds his helmet which rests on a fairly long rectangular shield placed upright on the ground; the other holds on his shoulder, in the manner of a pike, an object of which one cannot say for certain that it is a weapon since the end is not shown on the monument.

We must, therefore, assume that the *myrmillo's* only protection was the way he handled his shield; this implies a fighting technique peculiar to himself to which we find allusions in the texts. Ammianus Marcellinus tells us of soldiers who 'cover themselves in the manner of *myrmillones*', waiting until the heat of the combat leads the enemy to uncover his flank. Perhaps one of the classic figures of this defensive technique consisted in placing one knee on the ground and watching, from behind the shield, for the first mistake on the part of the adversary. So much for what we can conjecture with any degree of probability about this matter.

The origin of the *myrmillones* is as mysterious as the exact nature of their armour. It is possible that the name was first applied to the 'Gallic' gladiators whose helmet was surmounted by a fish and whom the *retiarii* were supposed to taunt when they took flight with the words: 'It is not you I am trying to catch, it's your fish; why do you run away, Gaul?'

We know, however, even less about other types of gladiators whose fighting techniques seem to have been original. That is so of the *provocator* often said to have been armed 'in the Samnite manner' but who, as an inscription published by Garussi to which not enough attention has been paid suggests, may have fought with a round shield and a lance; and of the *dimachaerus*, who according to a recent hypothesis was probably not a special type of gladiator—the word probably meant a technique used indifferently by gladiators of several categories.

From lacuna to lacuna, it is the essence of the gladiatorial art that escapes us. It means nothing to know the various special types if we cannot, for each type of gladiator, draw up a list of his possible adversaries and of the fighters with whom he was never matched, and explain these distinctions technically. Even more, we know almost nothing of the reasons for which one weapon evolved, disappeared or was replaced by another.

But the scraps at our disposal enable us to understand that all the activities of the amphitheatre were based on a complicated system of affinities and incompatibilities upon which the interest of the combats depended. With this in mind, we should be wrong in thinking that the Roman public was only waiting to see blood shed; the fact is, let it be said without apology, that they came expecting a professional performance.

(*a*) A parade rather than an exhibition, this scene bears witness to the elegance with which the animals were presented. They were often adorned with finery and on one occasion the manes of the lions were seen sprinkled with gold-dust. Mosaic from the Vatican Museum. (Photo Alinari-Giraudon)

(*b*) Sometimes one of the animals matched in a duel was ridden by a man who was not, properly speaking, a combatant. The mahout shown here is without weapons, but he can at will control his elephant's charges. The elephant is free to face the bull, whose movements are restricted by a chain fixed in the ground. Mosaic from the Vatican Museum. (Photo Alinari-Giraudon)

(*c*) Tethered animals: a fight between a bear and a bull. Mosaic from the villa at Zliten, Tripoli Museum. (Photo Boudot-Lamotte)

10. Some of the characteristic episodes of the 'hunt', and circus numbers in the modern sense of the term (central scene). On the right is a swivel device mounted on a pivot, called the *cochlea*; manipulated by a man whose sole means of defence it was, its movement confused the animal. Bas-relief in the Sofia Museum. (Photo Alinari-Giraudon)

III

THE HUNTS OF THE AMPHITHEATRE

The spectacle of the poor and the gala of the ruler

There was not the same teeming multitude on the tiers for the 'hunts' (*venationes*) as there was in the afternoons. These spectacles, in fact, which had nothing of the hunt about them save the name, were considered more vulgar than the others and took place in the mornings—'from daybreak' as Suetonius says clearly—at a time when a Roman, either of the elite or the working classes, was busy about his own affairs. But Rome, it seems, had unemployed, idlers and tourists enough to make a good show at the amphitheatre, since at midday it became empty, as we have said. The *venatio* was a sort of substantial hors d'oeuvre; as a clearly defined spectacle it came into being later than the gladiatorial combats, with which it was almost always associated. It was customary for a *munus* to be accompanied by a hunt, the object of which, as of the ceremonial parade and the protocol surrounding it, was to enhance its brilliance.

From the end of the Republic, however, the *venationes* took on such proportions as, in certain exceptional cases, to constitute a spectacle in its own right attended for its own sake; they then took place in the late afternoon and no longer in the slack morning hours. Some, moreover, as the inscriptions testify, lasted for several days. Time was needed to massacre the hundreds, even thousands, of animals of which the historians tell us—and also space. *Venationes* were held here, there and everywhere, in the Forum, the enclosure of the Saepta and above all in the Circus, doubtless wherever there was a space more or less suitable for the projected show.

The *venatio* was therefore less stereotyped than the *munus*. Furthermore a distinction must be made between the great spectacular hunts and the morning hunts which became more or less routine. These usually took place in the Colosseum which had been specially prepared for the purpose. So long as the animals had appeared in the arena chained up there had been no need to worry about the safety of the spectators; but once this safety measure had been given up in Sulla's day special barricades had to be erected. Caesar even caused a ditch to be dug right round the arena to prevent the elephants from charging into the crowd.

But at the Colosseum this precaution was unnecessary; the front wall of the *podium*, which rose to a height of 13 feet, was a solid rampart which, being completely smooth, offered no purchase for claws. Moreover an ingenious system of continually moving rollers prevented the beasts from gaining a foothold and, as a last safety measure, nets were strung to prevent the big cats from leaping into the crowd. These certainly hindered the view, already a little obstructed by the poles supporting the *velarium*, but at least allowed the spectators to feel secure.

The Colosseum also introduced other precautions specially designed to simplify the entry of the animals into the arena. It was no easy task to let a hundred or so untamed lions enter at the same time. They were not allowed to enter by the doors. They were kept out of sight of the public in vast cellars until the show began, when the cages by then assembled in the cellars encircling the arena were lifted by a system of pulleys into boxes embedded in the wall of the *podium*. It may be assumed that, once a cage was opened, the trap which had been raised fell back again behind the animal, cutting off all ways of retreat; and it sometimes happened that the animal, seized with panic at the bare sand and the noise of the massed crowd, after vainly trying to run away, remained crouched in the recess of the box, whence employees (*magistri*) specially entrusted with this task drove them out with blazing straw.

These men, who are sometimes represented, whip in hand,

alongside the 'hunters' (*venatores*), with whom they should not be confused, must have been able to escape unforeseen attack by closing behind them the doors of little huts resting against the wall of the *podium*. They were also entrusted with the still more difficult task of 'recovering' the animals after the fights for, as we shall see, not all of them were necessarily killed.

The one unchanging feature of the *venatio* was that animals always appeared in it; but their fate depended on the role they were called upon to play and this was subject to a great many variations. No other type of Roman spectacle had so many forms. Let the exhibitions serve as a reminder. Caesar won great renown for producing a giraffe for the first time in Rome. Augustus, in order to satisfy the taste of his fellow citizens for the bizarre and monstrous, made it a rule to display in the Forum unknown species sent to him by foreign rulers or by the governors of frontier provinces. All the same these exhibitions played but little part in the spectacles, for the good reason that, owing to the relentless pursuit of all species to the very frontiers of the then known world, there was soon no Roman who would have been astonished even when faced with a seal. Other things were needed to entertain them besides vague time-honoured feelings; from the very first it became customary to have recourse, here as elsewhere, to blood.

First, that of the beasts; they were matched with one another in murderous combats. Then that of men also. In this connection, we must draw a very clear distinction between two very different forms of the *venatio*. First there was a form of this spectacle— that closest to a 'hunt'—in which men provided with offensive weapons, and specially trained for this form of combat, generally called *venatores*, were made to fight wild beasts; then there was the well-known 'spectacle' in which men condemned to death, who were not necessarily Christians, were thrown to the beasts without defence of any sort and without any resource other than the recommendation to gesticulate, when they could, in order to draw upon themselves the attention of some hesitant lion or tiger. This last form of the *venatio* had, therefore, nothing in common with the first; the condition (however one takes the word, whether in its human or its legal connotation) of the men who took part, as well as certain details of its organization, made it a quite distinct spectacle, which will be discussed later.

However, blood did not always flow in the hunts. The existence of huge menageries at Rome favoured the creation of a real zoological garden, containing animals trained to perform the most varied tricks. And the habit developed of making them show off these tricks in the arena. Thus the *venatio* ended by including, in addition to the mass massacres and scenes of carnage worthy of the jungle, when all sorts of animals confronted one another, anodyne attractions identical to those of our own circuses. The Romans, naturally, did not draw the very clear distinction between these different forms which we are forced to adopt. The *venatio* was complete in itself and the public appreciated as a novelty whatever the emperors, anxious to surpass their predecessors, inserted into a framework which had long been fixed and which had become a routine.

Meticulous reconstruction of the struggles of the jungle

Of the animals chosen to match one another in individual combats the rhinoceros was the one whose reluctance to fight showed the most character. It gave pride of place only to the elephant, whose thick hide it could not penetrate, but it made up for this by its whims. A long time was needed to induce it to charge. This task was entrusted those men already mentioned who, clothed in simple tunics, kept well behind it and now and again cautiously hazarded a prod with their lances. But the result attained was not always decisive; it sometimes happened that the animal, after a first ineffectual charge, would once more waver between fury and contemplation, or, more frequently, go back on its tracks once again and nonchalantly try the strength of its horn against the marble *podium*. Sometimes the public despaired of seeing the advertised combat ever taking place. The *magistri*, green with fear, had to intervene once more. But once its fury was unchained, not one of the great beasts usually matched against it could withstand its charge; neither the bulls it eviscerated like straw dummies nor the bears it threw into the air like puppies.

It seems that the most highly appreciated of these duels was the one in which each of the adversaries fought in its own manner, or when two big cats of the same species confronted each other. There were also 'pairings', which must at first have roused the emotions of the spectators to fever pitch inasmuch as in a struggle between two hitherto little-known types the result was quite unpredictable. But some things very quickly became the rule. Bulls, for example, could not withstand elephants, any more than rhinoceroses or even bears, some of which clung to their muzzles or their horns; the enraged bull, dashing to and fro in the arena, was soon exhausted by the weight of this cumbrous guest. A classic match was that of the lion with the tiger, the bull or even the wild boar, of which there were then many more species than we have in our forests. These two last animals, Claudian notes, had both 'tired the arms of Hercules', and doubtless, to see the one with its mane erect and the other with its bristles on end in a parody of Homeric defiance aroused mythological memories in the Roman, however ill-educated. The lion, if the monuments are to be believed, emerged victorious from these combats; he is shown seizing in his jaws the neck of his adversary so that the skin hangs in folds and throwing all his weight upon the creature's spine, half crushing it. Other combats were a concession to pure sadism; a pack of hounds or a pride of lions was loosed after deer and there could be no doubt about the outcome; this was only a test of dexterity, prolonged by the more or less protracted death throes of the mort.

Every effort was naturally made to break the monotony of these scenes which always followed a set pattern. As we shall soon see, the resources at the disposal of the Roman menageries were impressive, both as regards the variety and the number of the animals. Other than those mentioned, hippopotamuses, crocodiles, hyaenas, aurochs, seals and the many kinds of

85

panthers Africa or the East could provide were common in the Roman Empire. Only the tiger remained a rarity, for some time at least. They had, therefore, to fall back on unfamiliar combinations to revive the interest of the spectacles. And thus, alongside the classic 'pairs' mentioned by historians, we see on the monuments a bear at grips with a python, a lion with a crocodile, a seal with a bear, and so on.

New strategems were conceived. One of these has been described for us by Seneca; a bull and a panther were linked together, one at each end of a chain; trying to get free the two animals came to grips, but hampered in their movements by the chain, which prevented them from manoeuvring, they tore each other to pieces little by little. At the end of the combat victor and vanquished were equally mangled and armed men, known as *confectores,* killed them both.

Checkmate to Pompey's propaganda

At the games given in 79 B.C. by Pompey who wished them to be particularly brilliant a score of African elephants, similar to those which had put the Roman armies to flight, were lined up in the circus for the amusement of the crowd. It was not that the sight of their enormous bulk could any longer intrigue the citizens, any more than the fury of their charge could make the soldiers retreat. The Romans had by then long been familiar with elephants which had several times been shown in the circus. This time, however, they were to be matched with men. Perhaps there were some gladiators among the fighters; but historians are not agreed about this. But it was customary in the days of the Republic to make barbarians fight in place of the *venatores* which the *Ludus Matutinus* was not yet able to provide; thus together with the hundred lions intended for Sulla, Bocchus had sent skilled archers to hunt them. It was consequently the Getuli, a nomad people living on the fringes of the desert, who in Pompey's time made up the mass of the troupe. It was enough, as a safety measure, to surround the circus with an iron grille.

This unusual duel at first astonished and even amused the

public. The Getuli were skilled hunters and had a very specialized hunting technique; they threw their javelins, aiming at the lower eyelids, and the beasts, struck in the brain, collapsed on the spot before they could advance a step, to the great surprise of the spectators; or else they paralyzed them by piercing their feet. One of the elephants, thus transfixed by several javelins, dragged itself on its knees towards its adversaries and began to tear away their shields and throw them in the air. The public regarded this as a 'stunt' and laughed.

Suddenly despair revived the herd instinct natural to the animals; they charged as a mass against the iron grilles which surrounded the arena. These did not completely give way. Then, resigned and uttering woeful trumpetings, they dragged themselves into the middle of the arena, and died there after prolonged agony.

But the spectators were no longer in the same mood; rising to their feet, and urged either by a feeling of real pity or by the fright caused by the incident, they cursed Pompey, even insisting that the beasts which had not yet been mortally wounded be spared. Dio Cassius has described the scene in his own manner: 'The elephants had withdrawn from the combat covered with wounds and walked about with their trunks raised towards heaven, lamenting so bitterly as to give rise to the report that they did not do so by mere chance but were crying out against the oaths in which they had trusted when they crossed over from Libya and calling upon heaven to avenge them! It was recalled that they had refused to board the ships before they received a pledge under oath from their drivers that no harm should come to them. . . .'

Some have concluded from this incident that the Romans felt 'a sort of tenderness for elephants, in whose good temper and intelligence they found something human'. A somewhat suspect tenderness, which did not prevent Caesar from offering to the public a few years later a somewhat similar combat in which he matched a score of these beasts against 500 infantrymen. The dictator, it is true, had to the highest degree the gift of learning by experience, even were it the experience of others, and on this occasion took care to assure the safety of the spectators by having a ditch dug around the arena. In any case, it seems that he thought that the anger directed against Pompey was a reproach aimed indirectly against the general for the levity he had manifested in showing so little consideration for the safety of the public rather than the fruit of pity evoked by a hideous carnage. If this compassion had indeed been real it is hard to understand how a man like Caesar, so subtle in his calculations, so attuned to the fluctuations of his own prestige, would have risked tarnishing the opinion his fellow citizens had of him by reproducing very exactly a spectacle which had so resoundingly failed.

Elephants moreover always continued to be killed in the arena. But under the Empire they were no longer included in those collective massacres with which the generals of the Republic had dazzled their fellow citizens and which had become customary. The emperors, indulging the taste for profusion which had by then become traditional, had hundreds of bears, lions and panthers killed *en masse* in the arena. Claudius had the original idea of matching them against a squadron of the praetorian cavalry commanded by its tribunes and its prefect, an idea later revived by Nero. One incident remains in the memory. Under Probus, a hundred or so lions loosed in the arena refused to co-operate; they let themselves be massacred without offering any resistance. Some of them even refused to enter the arena at all and had to be killed by archers from a distance.

From the Nemaean lion to the technique of the corrida

These massive baitings, a historian writes, 'presented a spectacle more extraordinary than agreeable'. They became, moreover, of relatively little consequence after the formation, first in private and then in state training-schools, of a specially trained corps which made possible the regular presentation of combats in which men and beasts confronted one another individually or in small groups.

The characteristic weapon of the *venatores* was a hunting spear

reinforced by an iron point (*venabulum*) with which they awaited
the shock of the charging boar or the attack of the lion, but which
they cast at the bear in the manner of a harpoon. They could kill
a panther outright by transfixing it with a lance, and pierce a
running animal with an arrow. If they missed they were in an
awkward position; clothed for the most part in a simple close-
fitting tunic, they had no protection other than leather bands on
the arms and legs; the weapon in their hands thus became their
only hope of salvation.

Some, however, were protected by iron plates which covered
their chests or by fringed shoulder-guards similar to those worn
by the *retiarii*, or even by a complete suit of armour identical
with that of a gladiator, made up of a helmet, a shield and
greaves, whereas others wore coats of mail which entirely
covered them. In this case they had no weapon capable of keeping
the animal at a distance; they confronted it with a sword, at close
quarters. They can be seen on a monument, kneeling to await an
adversary, sword pointing upward and shield before them,
slashing an erect lion before them, on the point of closing its
jaws, or a bear clinging to the shield with all its weight, ready to
crush them.

It has been held that a clear distinction must be made between
these heavily armed men and those who, clothed in simple
tunics, have in their hands only a single weapon with which to
defend themselves, and a relation has been established between
these contrasts, very noticeable on the monuments, and the fact
that there were two different words to designate the hunters in
the amphitheatre. The first are said to have been the *venatores*,
volunteers who fought with a noble weapon, and the second the
bestiarii, that is to say common-law criminals whose occupation
was, in Roman eyes, the lowest which the amphitheatre had to
offer. But conceived in this manner, the distinction appears to
have little substance. The term *bestiarius*, which was sometimes
used of volunteers but also of those condemned to be thrown to
the beasts, of whom we shall have more to say later on, seems to
have been a pejorative of very general application rather than a

precise label and if there was a very clear difference between *venatores* and *bestiarii* nothing proves to us that it should be interpreted in this way.

From the dramatic as well as the human viewpoint doubtless, there is a striking contrast between the men forced almost naked to face the onrush of the great carnivores and those whose armour gave them both weight and protection against lesser, paralysing wounds. But if we look more closely at the monuments it becomes clear that there is, in practice, very little to it. Spanning these two extreme types of 'hunters' are many intermediate types. We are therefore inclined rather to believe that this contrast merely displays two varieties among the large number of fighting techniques; and this is the more probable in that the risks run during the contest, though different, were equal. For if the man had no armour, his pike or his lance enabled him to keep the animal at a distance; if, on the contrary, he was well protected he would have had to brave the dangers of a fight at close quarters in order to reach the animal with a sword.

To tell the truth, fighting techniques were very numerous. There were even men whose specialty was fighting with bare hands; they would stun a bear with a blow of the fist and seize it in their arms, or choke a lion by plunging an arm into its throat while gripping its tongue with the other hand. Others protected themselves by using a bundle of reeds whose points prevented the animals from approaching, or rollers which they manœuvred on the ground, or a special instrument known as a *cochlea*, rather similar to our revolving doors, behind which the *venator*, turning the battens to one side or the other, could dodge the claws of his adversary.

To the various kinds of individual combat were added the *missiones passivae* in which of the most varied animals were loosed against a group of hunters. Sometimes, it seems, they were chained together as in the combats between beasts already mentioned. Sometimes, too, the hunter was mounted on an animal which was matched against another; perched on a bull or an elephant, he used it to disembowel or trample down one of the big cats.

In this extreme profusion the only combats which we know fairly well are the bullfights. As in our *corridas* the beasts were first goaded in order to enrage them; they were burned with torches, pricked with goads or dummies stuffed with straw were waved in front of them. These preliminaries were the task of the *succursores*. The *taurarii* or *taurocentae* were the fighters properly speaking. Sometimes they confronted the bull on foot, armed with a lance with which they had to transfix it, or with a pike with which they awaited it standing.

But besides these slaughters similar to those in which the big cats took part there were also real bullfights introduced at Rome by Caesar and of which we still find mention under Claudius and Nero. These involved feats of skill and strength making use of a technique borrowed from the Thessalians; the man, who had no weapon other than his muscles, mounted on horseback close raced the bull at full gallop to wear it down. At a suitable moment, he urged his horse forward and, at full gallop, leapt on to the neck of his adversary; he held on astride and then tried, by twining his arms round the beast's horns and joining them over its forehead, to throw it by twisting its neck.

Fairground tricks embellish the slaughter

Some of the ruses mentioned above, used at times by the hunters to put the animal off its stroke and baffle it by unfamiliar opposition, introduced a comic element into the combat. But there were also spectacles in which laughter was the main attraction and in which the *venator* appeared in the role of an acrobat, a clown or a tamer of beasts. One would enclose himself in a round basket which the disconcerted bear would push before it like a rolled-up hedgehog; others deceived the animal as it was about to seize its prey by turning cartwheels alongside it, or by disappearing into a sort of well or with the aid of a vaulting-pole darting far out of its reach; by this means they would leap over their pursuer which then had to make a sudden about-turn.

Among such spectacles, however, the most common were the 'numbers' performed by tame animals. Tigers let themselves be kissed by their tamers; lions caught hares in full flight and made it a point of honour to seize them gently in their jaws without a scratch; bulls lay on their backs displaying their bellies as their masters rode at them in chariots at full speed.

Nothing, however, equalled the prodigies of the docile elephants; they knew how to imitate the combats of the gladiators, how to take their seats at a banquet without overturning the tables and how, four at a time, carefully to carry on a litter one of their number representing a woman after childbirth, to say nothing of the regular tricks for which they were first trained, such as the Pyrrhic dance or walking the tightrope. These animals had such a reputation in Rome that it was reported that one of them, after having been scolded one day for its poor performance, was found at night practising alone.

Such spectacles gave the Romans a respite from the sight of human blood. Sometimes, none the less, it flowed also in the hunts. Doubtless the *venator* was not subjected to the cruel law which required that the gladiatorial combats should end in death (unless the public exercised its prerogative of mercy in favour of the vanquished). But we should be wrong to believe, as has been said, that the *venatores* ran almost no risk in the encounters we have described.

Epitaphs, and the scenes represented on the monuments which have come down to us, prove the contrary. Here there is a *taurarius* who has missed his bull, but whom the bull has not missed; there is a man whom a horn has tossed high into the air, or whom a lion has thrown to the ground and is tearing to pieces. It was said of the beasts that in group combats they always attacked the hunter who had wounded them. Finally, certain fights could have left the *venator* with no more chances than the gladiator had in a regular fight. The proof is that in the time of Claudius or Nero the final exploit required of gladiators who asked for their freedom was to kill an elephant in single combat.

It was fame and the personal renown which he acquired

in the eyes of the public by to the energy displayed during the combat that made the gladiator feel that shedding his blood was worth while. That of the *venator* was more anonymous; in all this hurly-burly the death of a man was a mere detail.

Men thrown to the beasts

The exposure of criminals to the beasts was only one of the elements of the programme of the *venatio* which was held in the morning in the amphitheatre. In the provinces, however, this spectacle sometimes occupied an entire day, or even several, as in Lyons in A.D. 177 where there had been forty-eight sentences and where, furthermore, the event made a great stir because the condemned Christians were well known to the public which, Eusebius asserts, called for them by name. At Rome, executions were far more anonymous in character; the crowd was stirred only by executions of notorious brigands or criminals thrown to the beasts for unusual reasons, such as the tutor of Glycon of whom we have already spoken and whose story was common gossip in Rome. That at least is suggested by Petronius' comment: 'You will see the populace divided into two factions; for the woman and for Glycon's tutor.'

This punishment, the idea of which came, it seems, from Carthage, was at first specially reserved for foreign deserters from the Roman armies. It was therefore the most shameful of all punishments. It was later reserved for men of servile origin as an aggravation of the death penalty, and still later, when the persecutions began, for the Christians. The condemned men were called *bestiarii*, a term also used perhaps for certain professionals armed for combat against wild beasts.

A warder, whom a bas-relief shows protected by a helmet and by armour covering his whole body, separated the criminal from the group to which he was chained by the neck and stripped him of his clothes. He was then displayed to the public, but only those brigands who had acquired a certain notoriety by their exploits were given the honour of a herald. It also seems to have been exceptional for the condemned man to be forced to make a tour of the arena, as was Attalus at Lyons, preceded by a tablet bearing the inscription: 'Attalus the Christian'. Generally the inscription giving the reason for the condemnation was nailed to the column of shame (*stipes*). The criminal was then tied to it, his hands bound behind his back. This column was not always a simple stake fixed in the ground. Sometimes a dais, similar to that used in gladiatorial combats, was placed in the middle of the amphitheatre on which the stake was fixed and whence the victim, thus bound, faced the public. From this doubtless originated the expression *surrectus ad stipitem* (from *subrigo:* to put up, erect) which evokes that peculiar posture characteristic of men chained tightly to a vertical surface, head and chest raised abnormally; it may be conjectured that this device increased the 'suspense' of these executions because it made the beasts hesitate. Sometimes the condemned man was attached to the upper angles of the *patibulum*, made up of two stakes on which rested a cross-bar; thus the body sagged and was pulled down by its weight. To make the list complete, one would have to describe a whole arsenal of crosses.

Then the beasts were loosed. They came on the scene in accordance with a fixed programme, but there is nothing to show that the spectators were informed of it. They entered the arena through trap-doors at ground level. Contrary to the popular notion, they were not housed there; the basement of the Colosseum was arranged in such a way that at the right moment nothing more was needed than to raise the cages of the animals lodged in the cells of the basement by a system of chains and pulleys. By a refinement of macabre engineering, the beasts remained in the amphitheatre only long enough for them to finish what they had to do; two underground passages leading from the cellar to the outside world allowed them to be sent back to their menageries at any moment, without being exposed to the gaze of the spectators. Before the spectacle they were starved, or else they had been specially trained to devour men; Dio Cassius tells us of lions and bears which were thus 'tamed'.

The bulls, whose victim was first enmeshed in a net, as was the case with Blandina at Lyons, or sometimes placed directly in front of the trap whence the animal was released, were first excited by fire or by having dummies thrown to them. There was not a region of the known world which did not contribute its quota of carnivores. The big cats, for example, which stunned with a single blow of their paws or killed at a bite, were less cruel executioners than some of the smaller beasts which dragged and tore their quivering victims in protracted torture; in Martial's expression, the victim no longer 'had the semblance of a body' and it was necessary finally to kill him off, as was done to all the victims at Lyons, where not one died of his wounds.

The statues were veiled, so that they should not be forced to look at these massacres. The emperor Claudius pushed his scruples even further; he was so avid for this type of spectacle that he made combatants tear each other to pieces to enliven his dinner (he often did not leave the amphitheatre) and in his reign, as we have said above, the reasons for condemnation were far from justified; a peccadillo, a calumny or a false witness was enough to send the incriminated slave to the beasts. Faced with this plethora of executions he had the statue of Augustus moved so that it would not have to be veiled continually. This precaution, adds Dio Cassius, provoked general mirth.

The public, inaccessible to pity, nevertheless did not share the enthusiasm of this ruler. Nothing broke the monotony of these massacres, save some rare incident on which the popular imagination seized to produce the naive legends and sentimental fables inevitably evoked by these blood-baths. It was said that on one occasion the lion loosed against a Dacian slave licked the feet of its victim. A leopard was then dispatched, but the lion devoured it. Drusus, who was presiding at the games, ordered the slave to be unbound and asked the reason for this marvel. Androcles then told the story of his life; harassed by the vexations and provocations of his master, the proconsul for Africa, he had fled to the desert, hoping thus to escape the soldiers sent to track him down. He had taken refuge in a cave, but had scarcely settled down before a lion had appeared, dragging a blood-stained paw which it had shown with a gentle air to the slave, begging for help. Androcles squeezed the wound and extracted a thorn embedded in the flesh. The lion then went to sleep. From that day on it became the slave's servant, bringing him the choicest morsels of its kill. At last, tired of this life, Androcles left the cave and was caught by the soldiers three days later; his master had then condemned him to the beasts. Contrary to custom, it seems that both the slave and the lion were granted their freedom.

But it was not every day that such an event occurred. Artifices had to be found to vary and give intensity to the spectacle. Weapons were given to the condemned men to prolong their agonies. Finally, the executions were integrated into dramas in which the denouement was death by the beasts. But this taste for fable, and the setting which it required, turned these dramas into spectacles of a completely different 'type', of which we shall have more to say later.

A pogrom at Lyons; the martyrdom of Blandina

There can be no question here of recalling the history of the persecution of the Christians, which has given rise to so many controversies and legends, or even of analysing in detail the causes of a conflict subject to so many vicissitudes. As we have just seen Christians were not singled out for a punishment which had become a traditional method of execution long before their appearance. It was not, however, the only punishment meted out to them; some were condemned to the mines, others were beheaded, according to a more noble rule applicable to Roman citizens only, but to which there were sometimes exceptions. Yet this particular punishment remains associated with their name. And this is precisely what is so amazing; why were the Christians, guilty in the eyes of the state of a simple misdemeanour, sent to their deaths in the company of the dregs of society? For death by the beasts was the vilest, most infamous punishment, reserved for brigands and slaves. Why this need to humiliate what one wished to destroy?

11(a) The hunters of the amphitheatre: the *venatores*. The man on the left [is] armed like a gladiator. His companion, clothed in a simple tunic, fights with the *venabulum* (a sort of stake), which allows him to hit the animal from a distance. Bas-relief from the Kircher Museum in Rome. (Photo Anderson-Giraudon)

11(b) As a Latin author wrote: '. . . . the erect horns call to battle; but the signs of the bull's anger are in his feet. He halts in fury, pawing the sand which flies up against his belly'. A sigillated vase from Montans in the Saint-Raymond Museum at Toulouse. (Photo Yan)

12. Scenes of the amphitheatre from a mosaic from the villa at Nennig. (Photos State Conservatory, Saarbrücken)

The explanation which at once comes to mind, namely the satisfaction of a mean hatred dictated by religious fanaticism, must at once be rejected. It is commonplace to stress the tolerance of the Romans, the effects of which our eighteenth-century *philosophes* so much admired. One cannot accuse of fanaticism a people which, as at the time of the Punic Wars, had not hesitated to turn to strange gods, even those of the enemy; a people which had officially welcomed cults the most opposed to the particularism of their own religious thinking; a people indifferent to all beliefs tinged with pure metaphysics. Religion—no matter what religion—was, for the Roman, more a means than an end.

The very real tolerance implied by this state of mind ceased at the point where the integrity of the state or, if you will, the unity of the empire was brought into question. By refusing to honour the gods of the City and, when the cult of the emperor had become an established institution, to sacrifice to the emperor, the Christians to some extent placed themselves outside the law. For this reason the fate most usually reserved for them was ignominious. Regarded as conspirators capable of every crime against the collectivity, 'against the human race' as used to be said, and dangerous to the state, there was no hesitation in applying to them a punishment originally reserved, as we have seen, for soldiers who had deserted to the enemy.

We have little knowledge of the legal conditions under which the tracking down of Christians took place. The mixture of arbitrariness and legality, of slovenliness and rigour, which governed the repression would be hard to understand if there had been any law to define exactly in what the crime of Christianity consisted. It is more probable that the magistrates acted against the Christians according to their everyday powers, as they would have acted against evildoers of any kind. This would explain why persecutions occurred in sudden outbursts of brutal fury, of which the authorities were not always the instigators. Badly informed, instinctively hating men who differed in every way from the masses, misled by legends which transformed the Christian reunions into mad and criminal orgies, public opinion often took the initiative in pogroms. That is what happened at Lyons in 177.

In the disorder created by the second Punic War and for reasons which had something political about them, Rome had adopted the cult of Cybele which, according to the words of Graillot, 'with its disquieting mysticism, the enervating seductiveness of its rites and the delirious fanaticism of its priests was one of those which troubled the human spirit'. To this must be added, as another historian has remarked, its college of eunuch priests, scandalous to the Romans who considered castration a crime against the fatherland. The calculated rigour of the old religion could not be adapted to such excesses. The goddess was honoured, but from a distance; it was not until the Empire that she began to play a real role. But then this role became prominent and the cult of the goddess was, in certain periods, closely associated with that of the emperor.

In the West there were only two towns, outside Rome, in which Cybele was the object of special veneration, Lyons and Vienne, which sheltered a large Asian community within their walls. It happened doubtless for the same reason that Christianity had already firmly taken root there in the second half of the second century. There was no dearth of reasons to fan the hatred between the two cults to the point of explosion. A coincidence proved decisive; in 177 the Christian Easter fell at the same time as the *Hilaria* of the sectaries of Cybele, exuberant ceremonies with which, on the date on which the sun made the day longer than the night, they celebrated the end of their mourning.

Though no formal proof can be put forward, the origin of the anti-Christian outburst which ravaged these two towns must be sought for here. Embittered by the coincidence and strong in the support afforded them by the semi-official nature of their cult, the sectaries of Cybele brought legal denunciations before the magistrates. These had to be carried out. The Christians were tracked down. Few escaped. After six weeks, Blandina and her companions were brought in two groups to the amphitheatre and executed in conditions to which we have already referred.

The pitiless nature of the investigations and interrogations, the atrocious nature of the punishments, the exceptional nature of the sentence on Attalus—who as a Roman citizen should have been beheaded—the ruthlessness which caused the corpses to be exposed for six days to the outrages of the crowd, all contributed to make this butchery one of the most striking episodes in the history of fanaticism.

Faked hunts

The Roman spectator had a sufficiently well-defined taste for travesties, for fakes and imitations that could be seen through, to enable us to distinguish it clearly from the more banal prestige that grandiose and imposing stage settings had in his eyes. It seems that everything that parodied nature on the stage, and drew upon the skills of mechanicians, decorators and stage architects to create splendid illusions exercised, a sort of fascination for the public.

The hunts already provide a striking illustration of this particular taste for scenic reconstruction, for aping reality. Every effort was made to give them a 'natural' setting by transforming the circus or the amphitheatre into a 'beautiful and verdant forest', according to the expression of an eye-witness. This sometimes involved considerable labour. Under Probus, the soldiers were made to root up and convey to Rome a veritable thicket of large trees, care having been taken to dig up the roots as well. A network of large beams was then used to divide the arena into squares, in each of which a tree was planted. It only remained to cover the entire ground with a layer of earth and there appeared a shady wood which, when the time came for the spectacle, served as a baroque meeting-place for thousands of ostriches, bears, stags and fallow deer.

On other occasions the machines and other contraptions with which the basements of the Colosseum were filled, forming a little town wherein were concentrated all the back-stage activities, made such preparatory efforts superfluous. Thanks to the skill of the Roman engineers a forest was first made to rise from the

99

ground, followed by its inhabitants. This time it was not a pastoral grove but a magic forest, an imitation perhaps of the gardens of the Hesperides; the ornamental shrubs which composed it were covered with gold, and fountains between the trees sprayed perfumed water.

The *silvae*—which was what the Romans called this type of spectacle—were not short-lived fantasies fashioned by the tortured mind of some ruler. The monuments prove the contrary. It is perhaps not too much to say that among other things they represented one of the manifestations of 'a certain form of Roman feeling for nature', very well analysed by Grimal. That nature should have come to be appreciated only as the product of the culture and ingenuity of man is in no way astonishing in an essentially urban culture for which the flocks and shepherds of the ancient hills had long since become pastoral characters in an increasingly artificial form of poetry. It is probable moreover that these spectacles gratified a profound feeling quite on their own since they were not usually coupled with the customary animal massacres.

This really baroque taste for travesty found a more perverse, one can hardly say a more developed, expression in another very special type of spectacle which had close associations with the *silvae*—the mythological dramas. To begin with, their settings were, generally speaking, similar. They were, from a commonsense point of view, theatrical mimes in which the actors really died on the stage, suffering the punishment proper to the plot. These dramas, moreover, had a somewhat complicated structure, since they were a hybrid of several types. The existence if not of a plot then at least of a fairly detailed scenario that controlled their development linked them to some extent with the theatre. Some of them were, perhaps, no more than very loose and extremely simplified adaptations of theatrical successes. But for the most part they displayed on the stage the adventures of mythical or legendary characters. This point is not unimportant: 'Let high antiquity, O Caesar', says Martial, 'lay down its pride; all its fame the arena offers to your eyes.'

The marvels of the Olympians were in this way brought within the reach of all: one saw Orpheus charming the animals before perishing from the blow of a savage bear; Ixion attached to his flaming wheel; Hercules, too, consumed by the flames; and Dirce tied to the horns of the bull or perhaps, according to a fantastic variant, on its crupper, her wrists tied behind her back, serving as the stake in the struggle between the animal and a panther. Sometimes, indeed, remarkable liberties were taken with the biographies of the heroes which were 'revised' to make them more spectacular and to provide a bloody end. In one of these dramas, of which unfortunately we do not possess the complete scenario, Daedalus does not reach his destination; as he flies over the arena, his wings fail him. A bear awaits him on the ground.

As can be seen from their subjects, these spectacles were akin to the tragic pantomimes, with which they should not be confounded. But certain of their elements were also akin to the *venatio*, first of all their setting, similar to that of the *silvae*; secondly when they were not consumed by the flames, as Hercules on Mount Etna, or Croesus whose robe suddenly burst into fire, the actors were devoured by the beasts, which brings this type of spectacle into line with the executions previously described rather than with the *venatio* properly speaking. The men who took part were also criminals condemned to death and it is easy to recognize in the robe of Croesus the *tunica molesta*—the inflammable tunic—which those sentenced to death usually wore. From this point of view these dramas seem no more than executions painstakingly 'romanticized' with the aim of overcoming the monotony of the mass hecatombs.

The feelings which they evoked were no less complex than their structure. The few descriptions left us by classical authors will be convincing on this score; in the middle of the arena, resting on an unstable scaffolding of planks, rose Mount Etna. Everything, shrubs and rocks, looked the more contrived for the care taken to give an exact reproduction. On the summit was chained a man, half-naked, playing the 'poetic' role of the celebrated brigand Selurus, the terror of Sicily, perhaps also of Prometheus chained to his rock. But he was a man of flesh and blood, and one could see from the rise and fall of his chest that he was afraid to die.

Before the crowd had finished feasting its eyes on the spectacle, the mountain had fallen to pieces and the 'bandit' had been precipitated still alive among the cages of wild beasts, which had been fastened in such a way as to open at the slightest touch. A bear seized him, crushed him and tore him to pieces, till all that remained of his body was an unrecognizable pulp. Another day it was Orpheus who held the stage. A magic forest, like the garden of the Hesperides, controlled by stage hands, moved towards him. He advanced, surrounded by birds. As in the legend, with his song he charmed the lions and tigers which the best animal-trainers of Rome had trained to live at peace with a flock of sheep. Then a bear appeared suddenly to put a horrible end to this scene and its deceptive simplicity.

It is easy to see how these cunningly contrived surprises, these contrasts between the destitution of the criminal and the sumptuousness of the setting, between his isolation and the communal jollity of the crowd, similar in sum to the artifices sought by sensualists, gave death a zest which it no longer had in the amphitheatres. No doubt latent eroticism had some part in the attractions of this sort of spectacle; this powerful muscular man chained to a rock, that Dirce, to all intents and purposes naked, offering her throat to the panther's leap that she seeks to avoid, are sufficient proof of it. There was also sometimes the obscenity which was the attribute of the pantomime; under Nero the dramas went so far as to portray the fable of Pasiphae, whose role was played by a woman enclosed in a wooden heifer which was covered by the bull.

But in his description of these spectacles Renan was wrong in accentuating only this aspect. He paints for us a Nero, both lustful and Racinian, peering through the concave emerald riveted to his eye (for he was short-sighted) and striving with senile avidity to experience 'a delight till then unknown to him' from the expression on the face of the unfortunate woman bound by the hair to the horns of a mad bull. It seems true enough that women were sometimes exposed naked in the arena; a terracotta found in Africa bears witness to this. But it was not the rule; the condemned usually wore a tunic or a loincloth. The presentation of the fables of Dirce or of Pasiphae seems also to have been exceptional. Eroticism, or at least vulgar eroticism, is absent from the dramas in which the 'actor' dies in the flames, and these seem to have been the majority. Nor can one see any trace of eroticism in the stories of Daedalus or Orpheus.

One must search elsewhere for the perversity underlying these spectacles. It will, in fact have been noticed that the principle of these mythological dramas lay in the search for an ambiguity between the imaginary and the real. This is shown in startling fashion by the trait which consists in making the actor whose very essence is to *represent* perish in flesh and blood. What is found here, not represented but 'reified', namely, transformed on stage into a thing, is what belongs essentially to the domain of the imaginary: mythological legends or fabulous history. The significance of this special relation seems not to have escaped the classical writers; Martial, witness to the fact that these dramas 'offered to the eyes of all' the marvels of high antiquity, adds elsewhere: 'Nevertheless all this is as real as what has been said of Orpheus is fabulous.'

It is clear that every effort was made to imbue the imaginary with a power that would make it one with reality in the minds of the spectators. To do that, it was necessary to reconstitute the setting of the legend in the greatest detail. But that was not enough and could even drive the spectators to enjoy precisely the opposite: the pure pleasure deriving from the artifices provided by this form of theatre which in the manner of some baroque spectacles made every effort to outdo reality under the semblance of truth.

It was the death of the actor which fulfilled this very precise function. We have said that from a common-sense point of view the development of this spectacle aimed at conferring on the executions a sheen of which custom had deprived them. We see now that it is just as proper to reverse this process; the death of the actor was intended to give all this papier maché the cachet of authenticity which alone could suspend the spectator's disbelief. Daedalus flies across the arena; it is 'pure theatre' and everyone really knows about the strings. But he falls and suddenly the illusion is shattered. The tale in whose inherent fatality the spectator has been involved and the laboriously constructed setting lose their quality of fiction. By a mechanism analogous to that of 'transference' the agony of the actor confers on what was false a sort of *reality in the second degree*, the mystery of which excites the mind. It is at the same time 'true' and 'false', even as the actors 'live' and 'mime'. It is, in fact, a theory of cruelty for aesthetic ends. Though without drawing the right conclusions, Renan is correct when he writes that these dramas consisted in 'making art out of torture'.

It may be objected that these are subtle considerations when it is a simple question of sating a public for which the sight of blood had become a daily need. In fact one might be tempted to pass them over in silence were it not that, in certain emperors, one meets with the most typical components of the emotions felt by the public at these dramas carried to the point of obsession.

There is in the first place the care taken to use artifice, not however to build a 'fantastic' universe obeying the laws of fantasy and imagination but, on the contrary, to copy with the greatest slavishness the world men see before them. Here, for example, is Suetonius' description of the 'exterior' of the 'Golden House', a palace which Nero had built for his own pleasures. 'It was so large that it had an arcade with three rows of columns a mile long; a pool *like a sea* surrounded by buildings *which gave the impression of a town*; and moreover landscapes dotted with fields, vineyards, pastures and forests where a motley assemblage of domestic and wild animals of all kinds roamed.' But if, in order 'to live like a man,' the emperor required his palace to be surrounded by a miniature world, so likewise did he wish this world to be reflected in its internal arrangements.

We learnt in fact that 'the main hall was a rotunda the dome of which revolved perpetually night and day *to imitate the movement of the world'*.

As for Caligula, he had the most marked passion for creating eccentric buildings which were, so to speak, the 'word for word' illustration of an abstract idea, of an expression or a phrase taken literally, in accordance with a procedure identical to that by which a legend is transformed into actuality on the stage. For example, to give visual and palpable material form to the symbolic identity established by his predecessors between the emperor and the gods, he had the Capitol, the temple of Jupiter (whose equal he was especially anxious to prove himself) connected to his own house by a bridge 'which overtopped the temple of the divine Augustus'. On another occasion he had built on the sea between Baiae and Pozzuoli a bridge two and a half miles long, made up of a double row of boats which was then covered with earth, giving the whole 'the aspect of the Appian Way'. History does not say if he also planted trees. When the work was finished, the emperor, dressed as a Thracian gladiator, rode over the bridge, from one end to the other, mounted on a richly caparisoned horse, and was then borne across it in a chariot drawn by two famous horses, this time dressed as a charioteer. This lasted two days.

Historians have racked their brains to find the most polite explanation for this peculiar behaviour; according to some he wanted to rival Xerxes by throwing over the sea a bridge greater than that by which the Persian king had crossed the Hellespont; according to others he had conceived it 'to terrify the Germans and the Britons by the fame of some gigantic enterprise'. This last explanation is worthy of the Picrocholin war, and Suetonius, who is not taken in, gives us the last word on this story. By carrying it out to the letter, Caligula wanted only to give a *second* refutation of the prediction of the astrologer Thrasyllus, who, in order to calm the apprehension of Tiberius, had earlier said that 'Caligula has no more chance of becoming emperor than of crossing the bay of Baiae on horseback'.

Another similar obsession of the same prince consisted of devising 'live' anecdotes with the sole aim of deriving from them abstract expressions or entities to which their ostensibly accidental and artificial character gave a very peculiar humour. Thus, after having poured a special poison into the wounds of an injured *myrmillo*, he took care afterwards to prepare a label which he attached to the flask, writing on it, from the name of the victim: 'Columbus' poison'.

It is noticeable that cruelty plays no part in the first two of these anecdotes. They were simple insanity. In Caligula's instability there was a far deeper coherence than in the blundering narcissism of Nero. But this is not the place to appraise its significance. It is enough for us to show that certain forms of perversity, generally considered to be the effect of the 'madness' of an individual, also sought expression in the amphitheatre. It was as if the feeling for reality had been weakened to the point where men took pleasure in parodying it, and the state budget destined to confer a visible existence upon the gods for whom the Romans had lost any deeper feeling, or to put into effect a policy of great public works whose sole aim was to 'solidify' symbols.

IV

PURVEYORS TO THE CARNAGE

Pacific safaris

A historian has pointed out that it would have been possible richly to endow all the zoological gardens of Europe with the animals collected at Rome for a single great hunt. Let us recall some well-known figures: at the games given for the inauguration of the Colosseum it seems that 9,000 beasts were massacred and, if Suetonius is to be believed, 5,000 were displayed to the public in a single day. These figures, which the classical writers themselves admit to be exaggerated, none the less represent a scale of grandeur impossible to doubt. Other factors indirectly confirm them; for example the progressive disappearance of a degenerated variety of elephant which inhabited North Africa until its final extinction in the fourth century A.D., and the growing scarcity of lions in those same districts where, it is said, they had formerly been so numerous as to beleaguer native villages.

By staging these entertainments Rome modified the fauna of a continent. This is hardly astonishing since enough animals were taken to provide for the gigantic representations of the amphitheatre for about seven centuries. But it is something else that gives us food for thought: how could a civilization whose technical resources were limited carry out the enormous and delicate task of collecting and forwarding to Rome the hordes of wild beasts which took part in the spectacles?

The whole empire was the hunting ground; from Mesopotamia to the banks of the Rhine, from Pannonia to Egypt and perhaps even as far as Senegal, wild beasts, which became a real source of wealth, were tracked down. Hunting, which in the strict sense of the term, became popular only late in Roman civilization, ended by becoming a solidly implanted tradition, especially on the great estates, as is proved by the abundance of illustrated documents, some of which show its daily aspects, very similar to those of our own times. Witness the scene of a picnic shown on a mosaic of which we shall have occasion to speak later; the hunters, in a circle round a spit, have stretched between two trees, to which their horses are tethered, a large awning to protect them from the sun. The freshness of the wine-jars set in the earth, the busy servants, the relaxed attitudes of those taking part and the activity of the dogs which are leaping after the scraps of meat thrown to them, all evoke with subtlety the typical atmosphere of a pause wherein the hunters relish every moment of rest.

These local traditions had their importance, as we shall see. But when it was a question of providing for the needs of the amphitheatre, hunting assumed a special character unknown to our civilization; active and ferocious animals had to be captured alive, whereas the present-day sportsman is content to run them down and kill them.

This dangerous task was first carried out by the use of a whole arsenal of traps and snares devised by the imaginative peoples of the forests or the mountains. The lion or the panther was captured by digging a pit concealed by a wall, in which was tied a goat or a dog whose cries attracted the beast. It leapt over the wall to seize its prey and fell into the pit. It had then to be extricated uninjured; doubtless a baited cage was then lowered, into which it was shut. Pits were also used to capture elephants, but this ruse did not always succeed; it seems that these animals, drawn by the distressful cries of the victim, sometimes managed to get it out of the pit by aiding it with their trunks, after having partially filled up the pit with earth which they moved with their horny feet. In addition to these automatic traps, the use of which as a sort of bush-snare is not fully understood, they also made use of the lasso and of a 'trick' which does not seem to have been mythical: several jars of wine were poured into a shallow pool and after drinking it panthers became tamer than tabby-cats.

None of these procedures were of a type which would allow the capture of very young animals suitable for taming. For that, the intervention of men was necessary. Armed with lances and large shields they went to search for the cubs in the lioness's den. They snatched them from her by making her retreat step by step and then threw them to horsemen waiting a few yards away. Not far from them, on the banks of a river or on the sea-coast, a ship was waiting, linked to the land by a gangplank. The horsemen fled at full speed towards this refuge, pursued by the now angry beast. If they were pressed too closely they would abandon one of the cubs which the mother would immediately take back to her lair.

But this complex sport, which demanded very careful teamwork on the part of the hunters and a comradeship proof against any eventuality, seemed only a picturesque entertainment when compared with the large-scale beats, of which it was perhaps only an episode. These were real expeditions organized, with the help of local people, by groups which did not always return intact, judging from the constant repetition of such scenes on the mosaics, suggesting that these adventures were on an epic scale; a hunter lying on the ground under a bell-shaped shield which protected him from a lion or, bare-handed, facing the beast which he had missed with his javelin. In such a case his life depended on the speed of his companions' reflexes; they rushed forward, brandishing torches or weapons to turn the beast's fury against themselves, as is done in the *corridas*.

According to a Numidian technique, the prey was surrounded and driven into an enclosure of branches strengthened by nets. Torches were used to prevent the panthers from darting back or bounding too vigorously against the fences by which they were imprisoned. Then the different species were separated, since to begin with all of them, ostriches, antelopes and carnivores, were left to mingle in the panic of the first surprise. Sometimes, on the other hand, they endeavoured to drive the great cats individually into traps, through doors manipulated by men.

The animals were then enclosed in wooden cages reinforced by metal. Protected by the darkness in which they were intentionally kept to prevent them from panicking and killing themselves by dashing against the bars, all that they could do was to get used to the slow rhythm of the oxen which dragged the carts on which the cages were placed. In this way they could travel as far as Rome. But from Africa this journey was no more than a stage. All the animals were soon on the deck of a ship.

Even if the embarkation of ostriches posed no problem—they had only to be tucked under an arm—it was quite another matter to get elephants on board. Their fear of deep water was so well known to the ancients that the passage of the Rhône by Hannibal's elephants had filled them with astonishment. A scene preserved on a mosaic found at Veii gives an idea of these difficulties.

Standing alone on the poop of a ship moored to a quay, alongside a coast or on the bank of a river, a man with a wide cloak over his shoulders, frozen in a hieratic pose indicating close attention, directs the intricate evolutions of a group of men at work near the fore-part of the vessel. An elephant has ventured on to the narrow bridge linking the ship with the land. Its feet, with the exception of the rear left, are firmly held by a rope. A group of men standing on the bridge above holds one of the ends, while a second group, on the land, holds the other. There is no mahout to help its advance; its progress, painfully laborious, is controlled by the pressures from above which drag it on to the ship while those below ensure that it does not miss its footing. Shackles in front forestall a mad charge and, for greater security, the ropes on which the slaves on the bridge are pulling are made fast to the bulwarks.

We know little of the conditions for the care of the beasts during the journey and especially during the sea passage. The classical writers have left us only the image of a ship launched on the waves of the Tyrrhenian resounding in the solitude of sea and skies with discordant bellowings: 'A noise rises from the depths of the abyss; all the giants of the sea rush towards it; Nereus matches with his monsters the monsters of the land. . . .

A serpent on the yards slithers drunkenly, a lynx leaps on to the rigging sprinkled with wine, and the tigress casts astonished glances at the sails. . . .'

The imperial service

In the time of the Republic the magistrates who gave a hunt in the amphitheatre had to rely on the goodwill of the governors in Africa or Asia, who were probably related to them, in order to get wild beasts. These men, in their turn, applied to merchants or gave orders to natives skilled in the capture of wild animals, so that the persons interested had only to arrange for the transport of the valuable cargo to Rome.

Things changed under the Empire. The capture of animals involved gigantic expense and their transport posed problems too intricate to allow the state, which had now become the greatest consumer of these exotic products, to confide it to the hazards of private enterprise. A twofold apprehension, security and expense, prompted the state to assure its supply by creating a special service whose organization was like a spider's web centring on Rome.

The legions barracked on the confines of the Empire provided a suitable and convenient labour force for the capture of the animals. In fact they included units exempted from regular service for this purpose, as for example the bear-hunters of the Legion I Minervia, which had its quarters near Cologne. The provincial towns along the route of the convoys formed the second link of the chain. They had the task of providing shelter and food for the beasts during the stages, sometimes quite long, which had to be made to prevent the wastage to which the continual hardship of a speedy journey would have exposed them. These pauses should in principle not have been longer than a week. But the whim of the escorts sometimes prolonged them indefinitely, to the point of transforming this already heavy charge into a burden out of all proportion to the resources of the *municipia*, which were forced to appeal to the emperor to put an end to this abuse.

Finally, menageries were created at Rome itself. They were an indispensable institution. By permitting the emperor to build up reserves upon which he could draw according to his needs, they freed him from the hazards which had formerly caused such trouble to the magistrates about to give games. For it was not enough for the convoy to arrive on time; it was still more important that it should not be decimated. It may be imagined that the beasts did not always stand these interminable journeys very well. Their very slowness was a major hazard, to say nothing of the changes in temperature and the risks of epidemics. When the animals reached their destination they were therefore shut up in the menageries, either at Rome or nearby. The elephants from Africa were sent by river to special parks near the sea at Ardea, while another menagerie at Laurentum doubtless welcomed the motley fauna which the painters, at their risk and peril, sketched when it arrived at the port.

It has been calculated that in the space of fifteen years 3,500 animals passed through the emperor's menagerie at the time of Augustus. Of these, 400 were tigers, 260 lions, 600 panthers, as well as other animals of all sorts: seals, bears, eagles, etc. Naturally, the maintenance of these carnivores, for the most part destined to pure and simple massacre, represented a heavy charge, even if they were not always fed on pheasants as Elagabalus ordered. A whole administration was needed to arrange their transport, supervise their maintenance and eventually their training. The inscriptions have preserved certain scraps of information about this. The considerable expense involved was the price paid for certainty of supply, and the treasury, at certain periods, was so heavily burdened that the emperor gave away part of his menagerie as a present to individuals.

If it were possible to calculate the total expense of the slaughter of a lion in the very centre of Rome, from the cost price of the animal to the reward given to the *venator*, it would doubtless amount to a very considerable sum. It is true, however, that this everyday act, which the natives of Mauretania carried out regularly to protect their flocks, was considered by

13(*a*) A man tied to a stake is pushed towards the beasts. Mosaic from the
villa at Zliten, Tripoli Museum. (Photo Boudot-Lamotte)

13(*b*) A man driven by blows of the whip towards the beasts. It is thought
that in this case the victim was a prisoner from the Sahara. Mosaic from the
villa at Zliten, Tripoli Museum. (Photo Boudot-Lamotte)

14. The vaults of the Colosseum, whence rose 'manufactured death'. (Photo Boudot-Lamotte)

the Romans as the symbol of their complete power over the universe.

The African wild beast market

The requirements of the dignitaries and magistrates who, throughout the Empire, offered their fellow citizens the spectacle of a hunt had still to be satisfied. Certainly, in the provincial entertainments there sometimes appeared only those local beasts easy to capture in the forests or on the mountains of Europe: wolves, stags, boars or bulls. But the great cats were also shown and were the more appreciated as a real luxury. So there were merchants who, save for the lions and elephants of which the emperor reserved the monopoly, had the task of satisfying this demand. Africa was the favoured land because of the richness and variety of its fauna and also because of certain special circumstances.

Unlike the gladiatorial games in their original form the 'hunts' which were introduced late into Rome never had the character of a rite. In the *venatio* proper, that is to say the fight between the *venatores* and a ferocious animal, the very fact that the issue of the combat was uncertain made any consecration difficult. The accomplishment of the rite would have depended on chance. As for the executions by the beasts, they were no more than assembly-line assassinations.

This was not the case at Carthage, where this last form of spectacle was used to satisfy the demands of a local ritual. The African Saturn, in effect the heir of Baal Hammon, demanded human sacrifices, which Roman law had strictly forbidden; the degraded form of the *venatio* represented by condemnation to the beasts made it possible to satisfy the moralizing demands of the victor without depriving the god of the blood that he required; it was enough to disguise the condemned men as priests of Saturn and to consecrate them to this god before throwing them to the beasts. This spectacle, which in Rome was intended merely to fill the gaps in the programme, became in these circumstances a real ceremony. The sacrifice was to some degree 'in the Roman manner', for it perverted an institution against

H

which the victor could hardly take strong measures, since it had been borrowed from him. None the less, in the typically Roman setting of the amphitheatre, a Carthaginian rite was celebrated in honour of a Carthaginian god.

This special circumstance doubtless contributed to the exceptional popularity of the *venatio* in Africa, to which so many facts testify. It seems that these combats in the amphitheatre were endowed with a passionate character which they did not have elsewhere; in the *spoliarium* of the great amphitheatre at Carthage to which the bodies of the *venatores* killed in combat were sent, have been found a large number of the stereotyped curses, calling down misfortune on the hunter's head in the hope that he would be wounded or be unable to cast his net. The combats, furthermore, were not anonymous, for the animals bore names well known to the public; bears were called Leander, Crudelis or Omicida. We find these names on the mosaics on which those who had given the games were not averse to perpetuating their memory. This fashion, much in vogue in the middle of the third century, bears witness to the public prestige of the hunts.

There was, in fact, in Africa a demand and the means of supplying it. The amphitheatre supported a prosperous trade which was in the hands of associations, whose number astonishes modern historians: the Pentasii, the Synematii, the Tauriscii and above all the Telegenii, whose name recurs several times in the inscriptions. These associations, more or less closely linked to the proprietors of the stud-farms, possessed menageries which it was doubtless easy to keep supplied by exchanging trinkets and manufactured products for animals with the natives of the frontiers. If one is to believe Biagio Pace, some of the rock paintings found in North Africa and the Sahara were probably done by these men in the evenings of the difficult stages which brought the convoys slowly towards the prosperous cities.

As well as animals these associations lent to the organizers of the games the skilled 'hunters' that they needed, thus playing a role analogous to that of the *lanista*. Perhaps it was their members, covered with medals, who are shewn in a banquet scene which has been preserved. In any case the Roman art of Africa bears witness to the vitality of these organizations; we find their name on a terracotta vase, on a series of wine-jugs accompanied by the exclamation *Nika!* (Victory!), and even on the mosaics. In this field we have a first-class source discovered about twenty years ago in Sicily, at Piazza Armerina.

Defence and illustration of the ancient world

As we emerge from the scorched lands we follow the slopes of a little valley where the almost transparent greens suddenly recall the ports of Tuscany forgotten for thousands of miles. We set off again, a little intrigued by a woman in a bikini, perhaps a dancer, if one is to believe Biagio Pace, whose book includes a very learned history of the bathing suit in ancient times. Perhaps it is not mere frivolity that attracts the tourist to this mosaic, in a style, it is true, less refined than the others. In the silhouette of this woman—a blend of maturity and youthful grace—there is an ill-defined modernity which is not entirely accounted for by the bathing suit (too tight to conceal an evidently satisfied stomach, like those exposed to the sun over miles of beaches between Taormina and Catania) or by the objects she is clutching to her. These are not dumb-bells, as one is tempted to think, but musical instruments, like castanets joined together by a rod.

There are about 4,200 square yards of these mosaics, of a somewhat similar nature and technique to those with which the great African landowners decorated their houses. These expanses of incredible wealth correspond to a specific need, excellently defined by Gilbert Charles-Picard in his 'Roman mosaics in North Africa' published in the *Gazette des Beaux-Arts* in 1958 as having given birth to 'an art-form typical of imperial Rome, whose aim was to enrich the huge houses conceived by the architects of a fantastic universe where the citizens found gathered together all the wonders of the world'.

In effect, the uproar in the heavens, the legends and the mythology formerly invented by the Greeks mingle there with the everyday delights of the age in a sort of 'mirror of the world':

Ulysses stupefies the Cyclops in his cave, Hercules dressed in the lion's skin receives the honours of an apotheosis, a Nereid and and an old Triton surrounded by little Cupids gambol in an over-peopled sea. In another place, maid-servants respectfully hold out rich robes to the mistress of the house as she completes her toilette, children play—one might say at hopscotch—servants massage men after the bath while others, ceremonially ranked, welcome the master on his return. Farther on, the Titans, halted in their assault on heaven by poisoned arrows, writhe bleeding in poses clearly influenced by sculpture and which make their serpents' tails still more dramatic. These are only some examples. It would take several pages to draw up a complete catalogue, which would naturally include several erotic scenes.

In this 'digest' which was perhaps intended as a defence and an illustration of the pagan world against victorious Christianity, the games, because of their everyday importance, have a leading place. Other than the chariot races, which for the moment do not interest us, hunting scenes of a most curious type are represented: children, dressed as *venatores*, confront small animals; one, according to the best traditions, has driven his javelin into the heart of a hare; another has caught a frantically struggling goose in his lassoo. Less fortunate contestants are bitten in the calf or trodden underfoot by a ferocious cock.

One's first impression, on looking at these scenes, is of a parody of the hunts, a fantasy similar to that of the Cupids taking the part of gladiators. There is, moreover, at Piazza Armerina a really clownish illustration of the games: racing chariots drawn by geese. But the realism of these scenes of combat seems to exclude any interpretation of this sort. According to some, these pictures illustrate an aristocratic sport which took place in the amphitheatre and gave the senators the opportunity to have their children admired by the populace.

As well as this mosaic, there is one of direct interest to us, the so-called mosaic 'of the great hunt', which strikingly depicts the details of one of those expeditions to capture wild animals of which we have just spoken.

An epic in a corridor

On a long rectangular band set round a central design are depicted all the various episodes of the hunting expeditions already described. The composition is simple. On both sides of a tongue of land which may represent either the headland of a continent or an island, two ships of different types are moored, symmetrically placed to east and west. Under the supervision of two officials, animals are being disembarked along gangplanks, while on the seaboard sides of the two ships other animals are being embarked. The scene marks the end of a long voyage which is the subject of the painting. Its various stages, starting from the places where the animals have been captured on the edges of the fresco, unfold in two long convoys, one from each side, which converge on the ships, placed by a technique of foreshortening at their point both of departure and of arrival.

From what country have these cargoes come? From which province of Africa or of Asia have the two convoys set out towards a common destination?

Perhaps it is not necessary to pose this question and to admit—for there is no lack of arguments—that the artist, without worrying about places or circumstances, has simply illustrated 'hunting scenes in a distant country' as part of a series of paintings entitled 'the transport of wild beasts'. But the strict symmetry of the fresco, and the very special position of the ships, makes one wonder. They have perhaps been dictated by something other than the demands of the composition. Perhaps we are looking at a very definite scene—the disembarkation in Sicily, for example, as Pace suggests, of two convoys from different countries? What about the conditions in which the transport of the animals was carried out? How were they fed? Stages were obviously necessary on the way to Rome for numberless reasons of hygiene similar to those which forced the land convoys to halt in the transit towns.

Certain details lead one to think that two convoys at least come from different regions: the captured animals are not the same, and the transport ships are of different types. Above all, at each end of the mosaic two women are represented whom everyone is agreed in considering personifications of continents. One of them is black. At her feet are a tiger and that same elephant, whose skin is a network of wrinkles, which can be seen being put aboard the ship on the same side of the mosaic; to the left a phoenix is rising from its ashes. Despite the presence of the tiger, other indications clearly suggest that the country in question is Africa. The other, a white woman, accompanied by a bear, whom one may perhaps identify as Armenia, is unfortunately damaged. This deprives us of the one indication that could provide that solid basis from which alone research could set out and give a more concrete interpretation of this scene.

For there is little to learn from the controversies aroused by the personage, undoubtedly of high rank, and escorted by two officials, who watches the arrival of the carts preceded by horsemen on the right side of the fresco. It was first believed, not implausibly but without proof, that he was the proprietor of the villa at Piazza Armerina. The mosaic perhaps commemorates a hunting expedition which he organized. Or perhaps he was formerly a high functionary of the province of Africa, honouring by his official presence the arrival of a convoy of beasts required by Rome, the richness of which one of its accompanying personages stresses by a grandiloquent gesture.

This led to a search for the exact identity of this 'great proprietor', since both his dress and his appearance provided some clues. A flood of hypotheses ensued. For some, he was one of the tetrarchs, Maximian Hercules, who had been leader of an African campaign, and had built this sumptuous villa in Sicily after abdicating, notwithstanding that certain sources affirm that he retired 'to the south-west region of Italy', which does not tally at all. For others he was a Sicilian noble, and they even thought that they could recognize his descendants in some of the figures represented on the mosaic. It is simpler, however, to think that the proprietor of the villa, obviously a man of advanced years, wished, in the peaceful freshness of the Sicilian woods to recall—either for his own benefit or for that of his guests—memories of the hunts in which he had formerly taken part on the burning lands of Africa. As Carandini points out, the frescoes have this advantage over the proprietor—they still exist. It is more prudent to confine ourselves to studying them.

It is worthwhile to stress the relationship these scenes could have to very real events. But it is just as correct to emphasize their vague, almost wholly fantastic, character. Thus the landscape which serves as a background to the scenes of transport and of capture has a Mediterranean aspect out of keeping with the animals which people it. There are also scenes of fighting between animals, intended to break the monotony, which, despite the remarkable character of the design, do not give an impression of having been taken from life; it is difficult, for example, to be convinced by the panther which seems to want to struggle with an ibex head to head, as if it too had horns.

The mosaic-workers had themselves very often never taken part in the great hunts. They kept to patterns which recorded 'typical scenes' which they adapted, sometimes confusing the continents. This also explains the surprising similarities between mosaics, the juxtaposition of scenes of great accuracy, clearly observed from life, with other episodes blemished by obvious errors, such as the one which shows tigers in Africa.

Another source of error lay in the widespread legends concerning these hunts. Everything about the hunts favoured the growth of legend: their scope, the distant lands where they took place, the countless incidents arising from them. Above all, the qualities which they demanded of the hunters, since a single clumsy movement could place the lives of all in peril, must have been the source of countless stories which became embroidered by popular imagination. Doubtless this explains the presence of a griffin among the various animals represented on the mosaic at Piazza Armerina. It is perched on a cage in which a man has taken refuge and is persistently laying siege to it. Apart from employing thousands of men, the trade in beasts nourished the imagination of a people.

V

CHARIOT RACES, STABLES AND FACTIONS

The origin of chariot races

The Romans held that the races which took place on the Campus Martius on the occasion of the *Consualia* and the *Equirria*, annual rejoicings mentioned in the earliest calendars, dated back to the time of Romulus. Their importance later declined, as the popularity of the games already described increased. Doubtless they were originally races of horses, mules and hinnies; the *bigae*, or two-horse teams, came later. Ovid, in writing of the rape of the Sabines, has left us a description of supposed chariot races at this time, in which it is easy to see the anachronisms. But there is nothing to prove, as Georges Dumézil says in his book *Indo-European Rituals at Rome*, that the idea of chariot-racing did not arise independently of all external influence at Rome itself in the ancient times assigned to it by tradition.

The circus, on the other hand, and the perfected techniques which it required, was of foreign origin. It is astonishing to find on the walls of a recently discovered Etruscan tomb, which the specialists agree dates from the second half of the sixth century B.C., all the postures and incidents typical of the races which we are shortly to describe: a charioteer looks anxiously back at the opponent pressing on his heels, another has 'capsized' and his horses are lying helpless on the ground, entangled in their harness; all of them, like the Roman *aurigae*, balance themselves with the aid of the reins wound round their bodies. Doubtless Greek influence had much to do with the development of the

120

circus at Rome, but the role of the Etruscans seems to have been predominant; it may be recalled that the Romans attributed to Tarquin the Old the twofold initiative of marking out the circus and constructing the stands.

Are we to accept the view that, together with these techniques, the development of which we are shortly to follow, the Romans also imported certain religious factors connected with chariot-racing? The funeral games of the Etruscans took place around a 'mouth of hell', through which the infernal spirits communicated with the living and whose existence is thought to have been recognized on certain frescoes. Such a mouth of hell, inherited from the Etruscans, which had lost its special character and religious significance for the Romans of the historical epoch, has been found in the sanctuary of the god Consus, the most important of the buildings of the Circus Maximus, having the peculiarity of being underground. The god Consus was not, it seems, an agrarian diety, as the Romans themselves thought and as modern scholars for the most part also think, but rather a god of the underworld. The chariot races were originally associated with the cult of this god, even as the gladiatorial combats were associated with that of Saturn. They would have been a rite, 'whose office it was to exorcise the harmful influences emerging from this mouth' and 'to honour the distant heir of the Etruscan God of Hell'.

This hypothesis has been greeted with reservations, an account of which would necessitate long explanations about the complex and controversial idea of *mundus*, a term that in Rome denotes, among other things, this opening which at certain times permitted the passage of the dead into the world of the living. For some, the soil of Rome was 'riddled with the mouths of hell', which makes the presence of one such mouth in the circus probable. Others, on the contrary, insist that their number was very limited; indeed only one is clearly and definitely identified as such, the one *in templo Cereris*, that is to say within the precincts of the temple of Ceres. The claim that the Etruscan tombs are identical to the conical boundary-marks placed at each end of the race-track in the circus has also been contested. Its weak point is that on very uncertain evidence based on the interpretation of exclusively archaeological data it calls into question beliefs firmly attested by tradition, such as the agrarian nature of the god Consus. It has, however, found echoes; for example the striking analogy existing between the altar of the god Consus which was unveiled only twice a year and the *mundus* which three times allowed passage to the dead. From that has arisen the idea of a Consus 'symmetrical' with Ceres and like her 'a chthonic diety, at once agrarian and infernal'. (Le Bonniec, *The Cult of Ceres at Rome.*)

Let us limit ourselves to saying, without prejudging the question, that the chariot races seem originally to have been very closely linked to the agrarian cults studied by Jean Bayet. The Murcia valley, where the great Circus was built, sheltered in addition to the sanctuary of Consus, those of Seia, Segesta and Tutilina, all of them goddesses presiding over the harvest. And the temple of Ceres, guardian of the growth of the grain, dominated the actual slopes of this country valley, which was to have so exceptional a destiny. It is thought, moreover, that the goddesses named above are the most important in a list which has only partially come down to us; and that, to put the matter differently, the various stages in the growth of the wheat were represented there by as many deities, whose union signified the closed cycle of vegetation. There obviously exists a striking analogy between this cycle and the circular route of the chariots, the characteristic of which clearly is constantly to close in on itself—an analogy expressed in concrete form by the fact that the valley was *marked out* by the sanctuaries of the goddesses who formed the links in this theological chain. It is perhaps also possible that the sanctuaries of Ceres and Consus were at each end of the Circus, as if they presided over the beginning and the end of the cycle.

These interpretations of the races either as an infernal or as an agrarian rite are perhaps not irreconcilable if we are willing to admit that Consus, like Ceres, was a deity of ambiguous vocation.

It is a substratum of magical beliefs more than any others that the circus discloses, as do the gladiatorial games. For even if it is true that the cult of Ceres appears to us as 'religious', that is to say it appeals to a 'free energy' by means of which men maintained well-defined relations in which the games were an important element, the ceremony of the race itself can only be understood as a rite of regeneration and of fecundity, aimed at reinvigorating the forces of nature, or rather of the earth.

A tourist's impression

Thus the circus games were at first only a fairground entertainment in a meadow on the banks of the Tiber; swords driven into the ground served as markers and the earth as a grandstand. Later, an enclosure was marked out, and the meadow was divided into tiny allotments granted to knights and senators, who were thus able to erect ramshackle booths resting on a scaffolding of planks.

Under the Empire the circus was present everywhere in Rome, not only in the five buildings which, though sometimes put to other uses, had been specially constructed and equipped for the chariot races, but also in stables so comfortable that Caligula took his meals there, and in buildings of all sorts needed for the training and maintenance of a prodigious stud. It was present 'in the air'. Like the noise and tumult of the city and the swirl of the crowds, it was a part of the life of the streets which first of all struck the visitor. Here a man would pass, elbowing everyone else aside, puffed up with pride, loud-mouthed and trailing after him an interminable band of stragglers; he was not a dignitary but a charioteer. He was also to be met with, in his typical costume, among the vast populace of statues which encumbered Rome and which it was sometimes necessary to remove in order to make room for living men; his name, and the names of his horses, resounded in the narrow alleys and in the fashionable suburbs.

This contagion even affected the cemeteries. For example, on a tomb was inscribed: 'To Coecilius Pudens, partisan of the

Blues.' It was put there by some mother, in memory of her son, who died at nineteen. The uninformed visitor would not have caught the allusion nor would he have understood the meaning of certain phrases heard in the streets; for example: 'Even if you are a rabid fan of the Greens. . . .' These colours designated the 'factions', that is to say, limiting ourselves for the moment to a concise definition, the stable-colours of two of the teams in the chariot races.

Naturally enough, in the midst of all this hullaballo, the religious sentiments which could earlier have been discerned in the spectacle of the races were crowded out. But much more than in the amphitheatre religion had imprinted on the circus a visible, even though completely formal, mark. At first the races were most frequently held on the occasion of the games offered to the deities. Thus, perhaps from the fifth century B.C., they figured in the programme of rejoicings of the *Cerealia* or *Ludi Cereales*, given in the month of April in honour of Ceres, the plebeian harvest deity. But in Imperial Rome the sacred origins of what had become a popular sport were still evident in the conditions in which the races took place.

The Circus Maximus

From a raised point near the place where the chariots made the dangerous turn which sometimes decided the victory, the Circus Maximus, the most magnificent of the Roman circuses, looked like two long tracks of sand bordered by tiers which could seat from 200,000 to 250,000 spectators in serried ranks, from the *podium*, reserved for the privileged, to the wooden structures reserved for strangers and slaves which, as in the Colosseum, crowned the edifice. The Colosseum overwhelmed by its squat and massive appearance; here, on the contrary, the eye passed over the unobtrusive lines of a building which corresponded in shape to the depression between the Aventine and Palatine hills, the ancient Murcia valley.

On the sides of these two hills were the stands. They were continually being enlarged by encroachments on the arena itself

or by the absorption of nearby streets at the whim or the munificence of rulers and of conflagrations; the use of wood in a
structure of this scale made the ravages of fire even more devastat-
ing, since the Circus was not isolated from the city. It was
surrounded by booths in which merchants of all sorts, and even
prostitutes and astrologers, plied their trades. It was there that
the famous fire broke out which ravaged a part of Rome under
Nero. The emperor profited by this incident to modify and
enlarge the building, in particular by increasing the inner area by
the suppression of the *euripus*, that ditch which Caesar had had
dug all around the race-track.

At one end of this long corridor, alive with excited spectators,
rose a sort of arched rampart reminiscent of the fortifications of a
walled city; its grey and pink granite softened the harshness of
the white marble. The Romans at one time called it the *oppidum*.
Above the central monumental gateway through which the ceremonial parade entered rose a columned box balanced at each end
by two battlemented towers. At ground level were twelve gates,
their regular pattern broken by the faces of twelve herms set in
the recessed pilasters which tapered down to the ground. These
were the doors of the *carceres* from which the horses sprang
forward. At the other end the circus was closed by a hemicycle
pierced by a gateway, the triumphal gate by which the victors
went out.

From one end of the structure to the other nothing broke the
uniformity of the stands. The emperor's box, which dominated
the *podium*, had disappeared by the time of Trajan, to make room
for that egalitarianism of which we have spoken, a pretence of
course, since, for all that nothing distinguished them externally,
special places were none the less reserved for senators and
knights. There was indeed an altar, near the *oppidum*, at the foot
of the Aventine. But it was lost in the mass of spectators, even as
the memory of the goddess who inhabited it was lost to the spirit
of the Romans. It was the goddess Murcia, who had ruled over
this area when it was only a tiny myrtle-covered valley, down
which flowed a brook. As the myrtle was consecrated to Venus,

Murcia had ended by becoming confounded with that goddess and it was Venus rather than the ancient guardian of the countryside that the Romans remembered amid the uproar of the Circus.

Except in the busy hours, to the Roman who crossed it early in the morning to greet his patron, the Circus looked like a silent city full of statues and buildings of all sorts heaped up on a base covered with marble, the *spina*, which followed the course of the former brook (now transformed into a drain) and divided the race-track lengthways, leaving enough room at each end for the chariots to make their turns. In the midst of what at first sight was a nondescript array of statues of heroes, gods and goddesses, seven wooden eggs displayed their perfect nudity while seven dolphins, rigorously parallel, spouted water into a raised basin to which a ladder gave access. These surprising objects were not symbolic; an egg was removed or the position of a dolphin changed each time a lap of the course was completed. Thus the spectator always had a guide, a sort of score-card, to show the progress of the race.

An antiquated folklore parade: the pompa

These, however, were not the only details which betrayed the religious origin of the circus games; the races were always preceded by a solemn parade called the *pompa*, in which certain elements borrowed from the due order of the triumph were mixed with the most ancient customs prescribing the sacrifices. The parade started from the Capitol, crossed the Forum, and then, by way of the *Vicus Tuscus* and the *Velabrum*, reached the Circus, of which it made a tour to the plaudits of the crowd.

At its head, in a magnificent chariot, came the magistrate who had given the games. Even if he had been ruined that day because the factions had compelled him to accept an unconscionable burden, he at least had this consolation; they were not sparing of the honours heaped upon him. He was clothed in a purple toga, wore a tunic embroidered with palms and held in his hand the ivory sceptre topped by an eagle; a slave standing behind him held a golden crown over his head. He was surrounded by the

126

gilded youth of Rome, who advanced on horseback or on foot according to whether they were or were not the sons of knights—as if the city wanted to admire and make strangers admire its youth which tomorrow would defend its walls. Then came the charioteers in their chariots.

An incongruous procession of statues, behind which marched priests and consuls, closed the parade. Some, representing an owl, a peacock, or a thunderbolt, were attributes of the gods, borne on chariots decorated with gold and silver and driven by children who, as the rite demanded, had both father and mother living. Others, perched on litters, were of gods or demi-gods, some from the most ancient times, such as those of Ops or Latona, others better known. Side by side with these were emperors or generals who had been deified, Caesar and Augustus for example, and even those of particularly revered women, busts of whom were ranged on a double-decker chariot.

Between these two imposing and majestic cortèges came troupes of musicians and dancers; under the direction of a dance-leader groups of plumed warriors, clothed in red tunics with garish sashes, performed a rhythmic dance to the sound of lyres and flutes. This dance was then parodied in burlesque movements by a troupe of satyrs and Sileni who, amidst clouds of incense, waved in cadence their goat-skin covered rumps.

Tradition has it that during the whole passage of the procession it was forbidden for anyone, no matter whom, to show himself at a window, under penalty of sacrilege. It was also said that when the procession entered the Circus the spectators looked anxiously at the statue of the god who presided over their activities. If, as it passed them, it made a sign with its head, caused by some movement of its bearers, this would be interpreted as support for their plans or as promising the fulfilment of their desires. In the accomplishment of these rites the closest attention was paid to tradition: the children driving the chariots of the gods must not lose their reins or touch them with their left hands, or a horse must not fall during the procession, etc. But the deep significance of these prohibitions escaped the public and their viola-

tion no longer furnished a pretext for beginning the games anew
—a custom which had had to be controlled since it had given rise
to abuses.

In fact, for the Roman of the Empire, the *pompa* was only a
boring ceremony which delayed the opening of the games, that
is to say if it were not made more interesting by the provision of
some kind of novelty, such as the presence in the ranks of a giant
seven feet tall or more.

The races, tests of skill and violence

It has been calculated that, including the preparations, each race
in normal circumstances could not have lasted less than half an
hour. But in the time of Nero the statutory number of events on a
single day, formerly fixed at twelve, was increased to twenty-
four. To the already considerable time needed for the spectacle
itself were added the delays caused by the parade, the sacrifices
and the intervals, of which the most important was at about
noon. In order to complete a programme so heavily loaded, it
was therefore essential that the races which began early in the
morning should succeed one another rapidly.

They began with a drawing of lots. In every *missus*, that is to
say every event, four charioteers, each representing one of the
factions which enlivened the whole life of the circus—white,
blue, red and green—were pitted against one another, though
this was not an absolute rule. Four balls, one of each colour, were
therefore thrown into a double-handled urn through which ran
a rod supported on two uprights. The urn was then overturned;
below it, were four bowls, each of which received one of the
balls. Their position decided that of the charioteers on the starting
line; on the rails, by the *spina* which formed the backbone round
which the race took place, in the centre or on the outside, alongside the stands. The teams usually consisted of four horses, but
there could be two or as many as ten. They each went to the
carcer allotted to them, that is to say the horse-box closed by a
gate where the horses, pawing and stamping with impatience,
awaited the start. The signal was given by the president of the

15. Mosaic from Apamaea (Syria). This shows a real hunt. The Roman aristocrats and the emperor himself found means of identifying themselves with legendary heroes on such occasions. Cinquatenaire Museum, Brussels. (Copyright A.C.L.)

16. Mosaics from Piazza Armerina (Sicily). Scenes of the great hunt: leading away the captured animals. (Photos Boudot-Lamotte)

games who, from his box situated above the *carceres*, threw on to the track a white cloth called a *mappa*. The attendants at once rushed forward and drew the cord which kept the gates of the box closed; the horses leapt out, each decorated with the colours of its faction, and already 'to the heavy sound of the gallop was joined the light sound of the wheels. . . .'

Should the 'greens' or the 'whites' leap out like an arrow and win a considerable advantage over their rivals, the Circus at once resounded with the immense clamour of their partisans, who shouted rhythmically the name of the left-hand horse, exulting to see it at each bound 'grow larger in all its limbs'. But this explosion of joy was soon modified by a touch of anxiety which tugged at the heartstrings; the habitués of the stands knew well that a team which thus took the lead only rarely held it and won. Cries of warning were shouted to the charioteer; by forcing his team on the first lap he was courting its irremediable collapse. Neither shouts nor blows could then rouse the slightest spark in his short-winded nags, overtaken one by one by their rivals, amongst whom even the veriest outsider seemed to have found wings. That was a catastrophe as hard for the charioteer, who overcome by his feelings dropped his whip, as for the fanatic 'fan' who, crouched on his bench and waving imaginary reins in his hands, shared the discomfiture of the favourites on which he had betted heavily and which he saw suddenly transformed into a team of slugs.

And so, at this stage of the contest, the charioteers, in order to moderate the ardour of their horses, drove with the body leaning slightly back; they gathered up the reins wound about their waists in the left hand, leaving enough to allow supple play, the whip meanwhile hanging in the right hand, useless for the moment. They were less anxious to go fast than to be well placed, for the charioteer's art consisted mainly in hindering his rival without letting him do likewise. It was clearly an advantage to run 'on the rails', along the *spina*, which was the shortest distance. If one of two competitors running abreast towards the rail managed to gain a few lengths, he would fall back and break the impetus of his rival, forcing him to slow down and lose time, lucky enough if he could get clear and reach the outside lane. The whole race was one series of such manœuvres, so that the good charioteer had constantly to work out his own moves and keep an eye on those of his rivals.

His art also consisted 'in shaving the boundary mark as closely as possible' and there again his success depended on the position he had been able to choose or to preserve. The track, as we have said, was made up of two stretches joined at each end of the *spina*. Where they joined were the boundary marks round which the chariots had to do a full turn thirteen times running in order to complete the regulation fourteen laps or, so to speak, negotiate 'a hairpin bend' in the most advantageous position. The result depended as much on the skill of the charioteer as on the responsiveness and docility of the left-hand horse which led the team and was not, like those in the centre, attached to the shaft but only to its neighbour.

The charioteer who took too wide a sweep lost several seconds or even, if he let himself be carried too far towards the outside by his horses, found himself drifting towards the stands out of the line of the race, a clumsiness which at once called down the boos of the spectators. But to keep too close to the boundary-mark involved an even greater danger, that of smashing the chariot against it or having it overturned. The perfectly rounded base of the boundary-mark assuredly offered no jutting angles; but the chariots, simple boxes open at the back and mounted on two low wheels, were so fragile that the least shock could cause a catastrophe.

As soon as the fifth egg on the architrave had been removed the race took on a more brutal character. By now the mouths of the horses were covered with foam, the sand squirted from under the wheels and clouds of dust arose from the track although it had earlier been sprinkled. The charioteers, one leg bent towards the back of the chariot and the other stretched forward like a buttress, stood erect at the turn, throwing their weight back, with reins pressed between their knees ready to brake at any moment; in this position they were constantly turning to watch the manœuvres of their rivals. The race was most frequently won in these last few moments; it sometimes happened that the second chariot 'revived' and managed to outdistance the one which was already considered the victor; or even, something which always aroused delirious enthusiasm, some almost forgotten outsider suddenly surged out of the field and passed all the others, one after the other. In such moments the charioteers drove abreast, wheel against wheel, for the whole length of the track, whipping their horses madly to gain the half-length which might assure their victory. At this point skill turned into pure violence; each charioteer was no longer content merely to hamper his adversary but took the risk of overturning him by driving his chariot against him in order to break its axle, or of destroying him by whipping his horses into the rear of his chariot. To ward off this manœuvre the charioter so threatened no longer leaned forward but literally 'hung on the necks of his horses'. He had no need to turn round to see what was happening. He could already feel the breath of his pursuers and the rhythmic shock of their hooves shaking the back of his chariot. A few seconds later, if he had not succeeded in gaining a little ground, there would no longer be either rival, chariot or team, but only an amorphous mass littering the middle of the track.

In the lingo of the circus this was called 'to be shipwrecked', whether the misfortune, almost always irreparable, was due to shaving the boundary-mark too closely or to the brutal intervention of a rival. It was the most spectacular and most popular of all the events of the circus; so much so that charioteers did their utmost to involve their rivals in this manœuvre in front of the imperial box. For a Roman it summed up all the poetry of the circus; with a sharp, dry crack the fragile box carrying a man was reduced to powder at full speed: the overheated axle collapsed and splinters flew in all directions; the horses crashed into the sand head over heels in a clutter of straps or, seized with panic, broke away from the harness which held them. Before the final catastrophe, the charioteer had to draw the dagger at his waist and cut the reins which, wound about him, bound him to his team; if he succeeded in doing this he had a chance of emerging from the wreck merely bruised, his body full of splinters. But sometimes he was pitched out head first by the violence of the impact. Then he had no time for this simple act and, if the horses did not fall, was dragged across the circus. As he wore nothing but a tunic held by a set of straps across the chest, his only protection was a leather helmet, insufficient to save his life in such circumstances. But the aggressor did not always emerge unscathed; at the moment of impact his horses reared up and came down again with their forefeet between the spokes of the wheel of the damaged chariot which was turning in the air; they crashed down, their bones broken, whinneying with pain, and the charioteer, halted in full career, ran the same risks as his rival.

'Shipwrecks', however, were not always so dramatic. The chariot might merely be overturned. Servants, wearing the livery of the faction to which the charioteer belonged, then rushed out to catch the loose horse or check those which were dragging the chariot to the other end of the track, or simply to help the driver. As a restorative, especially prescribed in such circumstances, he was made to drink a draught compounded principally of the dung of a wild boar. It is said that Nero himself drank it readily, not wishing to omit any of the customs of the profession. In less serious accidents it even happened that the charioteer re-entered the race or, if Pliny is to be believed, that his horses did it for him; during the secular games given by Claudius, Corax, a charioteer from the white faction, was thrown to the ground at the very start, but his horses went on, as if unware of the fact. They took the lead and themselves carried out all the obstructive manœuvres of which we have spoken earlier and, putting on speed when their rivals were at their heels, kept the lead until the end of the race. It is possible, however, that they did not accomplish this exploit unaided. For alongside the chariots rode men of the same faction, the *agitatores*, whose role, of which little is known, was perhaps simply to comment on the progress of the race, for we sometimes find them equipped with a sort of megaphone.

A white line across the track in front of the judges' stand marked the end of the race. As soon as he had passed it, the victor drew up, holding the reins elegantly in his left hand and saluting with his right. A man of his faction then approached him, raising his hands, while near the *spina* a herald who held in his hand three strips of cloth of different colour waved a fourth strip, the colour of the victorious faction, and called out the name of the left-hand horse, the *funalis*, to which victory was due. A very ancient custom connected with this sort of event required the charioteers to leap down from their chariots and line up for the start of a race on foot once the race was over. Dionysius of Halicarnassus says that this custom was still observed in the Rome of his day. But it was doubtless by then exceptional. Usually the victor advanced towards the *carceres* to salute the president in his box which was situated above them and receive from his hands the palm or the crown; the more substantial rewards, in money or in kind, were handed over to him later.

These formalities were scarcely over before the public, whose enthusiasm and ardour had cooled, demanded that the spectacle continue, shouting: 'The others, the others!'

The circus and the Art of Love

Quite apart from the interest of the connoisseur which the public might display during these shows and the fanaticism engendered by the races themselves, a number of quite distinct circumstances combined, as Jérôme Carcopino has pointed out, to to give the circus its attraction: 'The swarming multitudes in which everyone was carried along by the crush, the incredible grandeur of the setting where perfumes floated in the air and toilettes shimmered, the sanctity of the ancient religious ceremonies, the physical presence of the emperor . . . the vicissitudes of the various events which threw into relief the power and beauty of the stallions, the richness of their harness, the perfection of their training and, above all, the skill and gallantry of the charioteers and horsemen. . . .'

In short, it was in this stately setting, in the midst of all the official pomp by which was made manifest the fact that this had been consecrated ground from time immemorial, that the crowd made itself at home. When Ammianus Marcellinus asserts that the circus is 'its temple, its house, the place where it comes together, animated by the same hope and the same passions' his words are not to be taken solely in a figurative sense. This crowd had the feeling of being at home. Here men found their own image, gave vent to their satisfaction at feeling alive and to all their natural lack of decorum. They ate, even though an edict had proscribed the taking of any refreshment during the spectacle; they called one another by high-sounding names which 'had an aristocratic ring', like Semicupus, Gluterinus, Lucanicus, Pordacus or Salsula. They even voiced their discontent and their demands to the emperor himself. They went so far as to disregard the most elementary rules of decency, if it be true that, pressed by a natural need, certain spectators did not hestitate to expose themselves indecently in public.

But above all the circus was the ideal place in which to carry an amorous intrigue to its successful conclusion. Contrary to what happened at other spectacles, men and women here sat together on the stands. Everything helped to make it in this connection a privileged place: the special excitement engendered by the presence of a multitude of women who came, as to the amphitheatre, dressed for the occasion and whose clothing and behaviour gave an illusion of infinite variety. There was everything. 'You will find there', says Ovid, 'some beauty who may seduce you, another whom you may deceive, another who will be for you just a passing whim, and yet another whom you wish to keep.' The crush and the absence of individual seats engendered a forced promiscuity, as did even more the feeling of being at one to which the anticipation and enjoyment of the spectacle gave rise.

There were a thousand pretexts for scraping an acquaintance; reproving the tiresome fellow who dug his knees into the back of the woman in front of him or into her shoulders, lifting the dress which was trailing on the dusty stone, brushing away a pretended speck of dust should the need arise, offering a footstool or waving a tablet in lieu of a fan, not to speak of the facilities which the race itself provided for sustaining conversation and dropping fairly broad hints in the course of the chit-chat accompanying a first meeting. The intrigue began here was continued elsewhere. 'The fair one has smiled and her sparkling eyes give a promise. That is enough. The rest is up to you.'

Four colours, one passion

To all appearances the factions were merely sporting labels. A man was for or against the 'Greens' as he is 'for' the Arsenal or this or that centre forward. Such allegiance was, in the first instance, purely personal, an affiliation based on a loyalty which did not necessarily imply any professional bond with the economic complex which each of the factions represented. There were four of these or, if you like, four 'stables', an expression which in short seems more nearly equivalent to *factiones* than the words 'parties' or 'factions'. To the oldest amongst them, the 'Whites' and 'Reds', there were added, doubtless in the early days of the Empire, the 'Blues' and 'Greens', whose rivalry ended by dominating the scene, if one is to believe the many testimonies handed down to us in literature. The purple and the gold factions, which were introduced under Domitian, lasted only a short time, for it seems that there was among the spectators a tendency to simplify the choice; the 'Whites' in fact later became merged with the 'Greens', the 'Reds' with the 'Blues'. They preserved, however, their distinctive marks, that 'colour' which glittered on the coats of the charioteers, the livery of the *jubilatores*, sometimes even on the sand of the race-track, and which we ourselves find once more on the mosaics.

The frenzy engendered by partisanship, which drove the Romans to support one or other of the stables, is well known. The writers of antiquity have given us more information about these manifestations than about the conduct and running of the races themselves. The craze was universal; it affected children as well as adults, slaves (permitted to watch the races and to bet)

as well as free men. It did not spare even the cultured; as
Friedländer remarks, a serious and sententious man like Fronto,
sick as he was, preferred to drag himself to the Circus rather than
miss a race. On race days all Rome was to be found on the tiers;
and Juvenal, when he heard the plaudits of the Circus across the
deserted city, concluded that the 'Greens' had won, for if they
had been defeated the city 'would be as dejected and dismayed
as on the day the consuls bit the dust at Cannae'.

Among the rich this fanaticism was linked with the most
unexpected follies and extravagances. Horses in Rome had marble
stables and instead of barley ate raisins and dates from ivory
mangers; others were pensioned off when no longer of an age to
race. Dignitaries like Lucius Verus maintained a feverish corre-
spondence with all the provinces about the health of his horses.
For some the official mail was not fast enough: the 'manager' of
a faction used to bring swallows with him to Rome which after
being painted with the colour of the victorious faction were set
free to announce the result to his friends.

On the tiers the outbursts of feeling took an equally picturesque
form. People fainted, their hands over their eyes, when a rival
overtook their favourite. They provoked one another with
gestures, insulted one another, jostled their neighbours, rose in a
mass waving the sleeves of their tunics. Others contrariwise
forgot where they were and completely lost their heads, to the
point of commenting in broken trance-like phrases on every
incident on the track as if they alone among the 200,000 present
had eyes to see—a phenomenon in which Tertullian, who already
saw the devil present in the square of white stuff thrown into the
arena at the start of the race, found proof of demoniac possession.
There was no one whose expression and colour did not change
according to the vicissitudes of the race, and who was not moved
by the most extreme feelings; and the end of each event found
half the circus prancing with rage and the other half transported
in a delirium of deafening cheers.

It is traditional to lay stress on the unwholesome and un-
intelligent nature of this passion. It had nothing to do with

anything that might enable such competitions to be of real value, such as the skill of the charioteers, and the power and elegance of the horses. It rejected all the values that sport, as conceived by the Greeks, pre-supposed. It clung with the poverty of obsession to a colour, to a charioteer's coat. That alone counted, and if, as Pliny suggests, the teams had changed colour in the middle of a race, the public would have forsaken the horses and drivers whose names they shouted, whose victories and the minutest details of whose personal lives were known to them, and would have transferred their allegiance to the others. The implications of such a judgement are clear; as we have already suggested, the passion for the races was more complex than a mania.

Men like Pliny the Younger, wholly concerned with abstract elegance, had not the slightest sympathy for these plebeians, whom they considered 'viler than a tunic'. They could not be expected to understand the sophisticated charm of the circus. We need for that the poetic sense of Ovid or the insight of the intransigent confessor which characterized Tertullian. But Pliny, for all that he simplified matters, did seize upon the most characteristic and perhaps profound aspect of this hippomania. Its essential factors were unquestionably partisanship and the insensate desire to see 'the' colour triumph. Men, in fact, did not bet on the horses but on the stable; nor, despite the veneration with which they regarded the charioteers, did they accord them their prime loyalty, since these changed stables according to the advantages offered them.

By a phenomenon of which there are few examples in the history of sport, the Roman citizen identified himself with an apparently meaningless symbol, a banner with no more reality than those of children's games, a *sign*. It is for the sociologist rather than the historian to analyse the mechanisms which can set in motion a process of this nature, common enough after all.

Let us say only, for the moment, that this sort of prejudice, originally connected with sport, had such wide repercussions in other spheres of activity that it must be regarded as a social phenomenon. The factions certainly were literally, as Maricq says in his article 'The Circus factions and popular parties', 'amateur groupings . . . kept together by somewhat loose bonds', but it is just such 'somewhat loose bonds' based on a common feeling for the same things, on meeting in the same places and associating with the same men, that, in short, are the strongest and that, in a society of real 'fans', can forge bonds whose effectiveness lies precisely in the fact that they are not founded on any definite institution.

Perusal of certain biographies leaves no doubt of the role which affiliation to a faction could play in a man's career—and here we are not speaking of the sensational and ephemeral advancement of certain charioteers. The career of the emperor Vitellius, for example, ran its course successively under the aegis of the 'Greens' and the 'Blues', between the stables and the race-track, the marks of which he bore on his body, having one day been knocked down by a *quadriga*. He had, in fact, originally worked for Caligula as a groom. He was then granted the governorship of Germania on the recommendation of T. Vinius, at that time all-powerful, with whom he was on intimate terms because of their common affiliation to the 'Blue' faction. On another level, the underhand manœuvres of the Circus served to turn a moderately gifted man into the most fashionable orator of the Roman schools. In this profession it was enough that he knew how to cut short the pompous discourses with which he regaled his pupils by well-informed tips for the chariot races. Naturally, the susceptibilities engendered by fanaticism could also produce opposite results and plebeians, poor devils who in no way merited the persecution of the ruler, were sent to the executioner for having criticized the 'Blues' in his presence.

Had it been necessary, recent archaeological discoveries would have confirmed this. We already know that the seats of the factions were real clubs where their supporters met. At Rome these clubs were to be found on the Campus Martius, and certain amateurs, such as Caligula, spent the whole day there. As Suetonius says, he 'dined and passed his whole time' in the company of the 'Greens'. In 1960 a mosaic of exceptional importance, owing to its size, its variety and the refinement of its technique, the mosaic of the House of the Horses, was found on the site of ancient Carthage. In this imposing ensemble, where scenes inspired by African magic lie cheek by jowl with other more classic ones, such as hunting episodes or Venus dressing, a whole hall is devoted to the circus. As well as charioteers and *jubilatores* it shows a considerable number of racehorses accompanied by persons who do not concern us. What interests us here is the 'colour'—one might have suspected that for an inquiry of this sort, mosaics would be of value.

They reveal to us, in fact, the 'uniform' of the factions as it was worn by the charioteers, employees and horses; at Douggha, for example, the charioteer Eros wears a helmet and a cap that are quite clearly green. But in our mosaic clothes and ornaments are all blue, with the exception of a red helmet and some red harness, which is no cause for astonishment, since we know that these two stables were associated.

To explain this riot of blue, we must go back several decades. In 1926 there was discovered on a rise a short distance away a hall which we now know formed part of the same architectural complex as the House of the Horses. On the mosaic pavement can be read in large capitals, in the centre of a sober and restrained decoration, the inscription FELIX POPULUS VENETI, or in slang parlance 'Up the Blues!' There is good reason to think that this strikingly rich complex was the seat of the 'Blue' faction at Carthage—one of those clubs of which we have just been speaking.

An apolitical mass

The beginning of wisdom, when it is a question of deciding what role these clubs may have played in political life in the strict sense of the term, is certainly to distinguish Rome from Byzantium and, carrying tautology to its utmost, the Early from the Later Roman Empire. For the factions everywhere followed the shattering successes of the circus; copying the Roman model, they are to be found at Carthage, at Antioch and at Byzantium.

But in the last-named city, from a date which cannot be exactly determined, the 'Blues' and 'Greens' no longer had anything in common with their Roman ancestors. They became real political parties, favourable or hostile to established authority and liable, when circumstances demanded, to organize their own militias; when menaced by an enemy, the 'Greens' protected the seaports and the 'Blues' defended a part of the city. They were popular bodies, like *demes*, and despite the similarity of name were in no way comparable to the factions of ancient Rome. The phenomenon had changed its nature. It remains to be seen what the role of the circus was in this.

Manojlović has pointed out that it may well have been that the parties were formed from the very sports clubs on which the circus had set the stamp of its approval, and which would have provided them with means of expression and organization. It is certain, in any case, that the hippodrome of Byzantium became something different from a race-course, a real forum where events took place which had nothing to do with the love of the circus and where, in the presence of the emperor, the irreconcilable enemies, the 'Blues' and the 'Greens', took their places. If in the thirties the Communist Party and the Action Française, forming armed and official militias, had suddenly monopolized the allegiance of the Parisians and divided it among themselves to the exclusion of all other parties, we can see at once what might have taken place at the Parc des Princes. The President of the Republic would doubtless have taken little pleasure in honouring the Cup Final by his presence. Moreover the two parties, in league at times, could have given him a rough passage. And if, on the occasion of some banal incident, they had begun killing one another, who would have been surprised?

That is what happened at Byzantium during the famous Nika riots on 11 January 532, in the reign of Justinian and Theodora. In the preceding days there had been a number of murders in the city. The 'Greens' were exasperated by the partiality of the empress, who had allowed the 'Blues' to sate their vengeance without restraint. Invectives began to crackle from the tiers of the hippodrome. Justinian peremptorily challenged the people: 'You have not come here to see the spectacle but to insult the government.' A dialogue punctuated by abuse took place between the 'Greens' who complained at being excluded from the government and the herald who was supported by the 'Blues'. Finally, the 'Greens' left the hippodrome *en masse* which was the worst insult they could offer the emperor. Next day, thanks to the blunders of Justinian and his subordinates, 'Blues' and 'Greens' joined forces against the Palace. This episode marked the start of a full-scale rebellion with masterly intrigues, uncertainties and exemplary punishments. There were thirty thousand victims.

On other days an incident relating to the races themselves could have been the spark that lit the powder barrel. But, as is clear, these bloody excesses were not, as has been supposed, the result of a sporting fanaticism which supposedly took on the proportions of a mental disease and dominated political life to the point where it could make or unmake emperors. The hippodrome was only the setting; the passions unleashed there were nurtured elsewhere. If one takes this into account, it is even wrong to say that the prejudices engendered by the circus reached the peak of exasperation at Byzantium. The frenzy that takes hold of the treble-chance fanatic and that which provokes the bloody fury of the partisans are not at all the same. We must not confound them.

The 'Blues' and the 'Greens' also played an active part in a riot at Rome in 509 and even though the history of the factions varied considerably from one city to another—for example, at Carthage we find the 'Greens' allied to the 'Blues'—the institutions to which they gave birth undoubtedly became progressively more political everywhere. This is scarcely surprising considering how deeply the circus was rooted in public life. But it is impossible to distinguish the stages and the forms of this evolution.

We can only say that from the very first days of the Empire the supporters of the 'Blues' belonged for the most part to the aristocracy whereas the votes of the populace were given to the 'Greens'. The partialities of the emperors in this matter are characteristic. Nero, Caligula, Lucius Verus, Commodus and Elagabalus were inclined to demagogy and arbitrary action and were heart and soul on the side of the 'Greens'; in the first instance, no doubt out of distrust of an aristocracy to which they were instinctively hostile and which they did not scruple to treat roughly; but also to give their tyranny the popularity that was its sole support, by flattering the tastes of the masses. The attitude of Vitellius is equally revealing; though attached to the 'Blues' he did not hesitate openly to flatter the 'Greens' as soon as he was in power, trying to curry favour with them as some of his predecessors had done.

But this partiality for one or the other faction shows nothing more than a simple political trend, a feeling for social conformity and, amongst the 'Blues', a nostalgia for a vanished world. It would be to misunderstand completely the nature of the regime in power to see in this very limited form of political action an explanation for the passion of the Romans for the races. It was not the fruit of political rivalries which might be supposed to have found in the factions a symbol and a spur. It was, among other things, the inoffensive form by which a people which had abdicated all responsibility expressed what little civic conscience remained to it. Instead of showing that the circus had become political, the facts mentioned above rather bear witness to the progressive lack of interest in politics shown by the masses, fed by the state and protected on the frontiers by generals whose distant victories they had grown accustomed to hear announced. The effect, if not the intention, of the races, as for that matter of all the games, was to preserve the lack of interest in and indifference to politics. This indifference may have been real or fed by fear; the circus provided the mass of the people with a subject of conversation which was the more appreciated in that it was not compromising.

A fact that should have been noticed is that the 'Greens' of Byzantium, in the conflict which ranged them against Justinian, had in the real sense of the term boycotted the races by leaving the hippodrome in a body. There was no danger of this happening when Nero presided at the Circus Maximus. At Rome the spectacle of the races made men forget. A few centuries later, at Byzantium, on the contrary, it revived social and political antagonisms. In origin, however, it was the same institution.

Symbolism and charlatanism

A symbolism of the circus was, at Rome, grafted on to the games in conditions which we do not know precisely. It was based on an exact system of parallels which have been studied by Pierre Wuilleumier in an article in the *Mélanges de l'école française de Rome* in 1927. The hippodrome was held to represent the world in miniature. The arena was the image of the earth. The *euripus* was that of the 'blue-green sea'. The obelisk which rose in the centre of the *spina* represented the ridge-pole of the heavens or, if you like, the apogee of the sun's course which it divided into two. Even the minutest detail had some significance; the gates of the *carceres*, twelve in number, represented the months of the year, and the boundary-marks, three in number, which, to east and west, marked out the course, comprised, as in the signs of the Zodiac, three decans. Nor have we exhausted the list of these parallels.

Naturally the factions, or rather the 'colours', found their place in this crazy architecture. They represented the seasons which, in the particular style reserved for this sort of thing by popular tradition, could be translated as follows: green as spring, the renewal of nature, Venus; red as summer, fire, Mars; blue as autumn, the heavens and the sea, Saturn or Neptune; white as winter, the zephyrs, Jupiter.

It is not very likely that this symbolism should have remained the property of a restricted circle excessively devoted to speculation. The assimilation of the factions to the seasons we can in any case find on the mosaics, where it sometimes takes the form of a rebus. The horses of each stable are associated in it with a plant which is itself the symbol of a season: wheat for summer, ivy for autumn, millet for winter and the rose for spring. Certainly the artists who composed these mosaics worked from pattern books which contained models and themes suitable for the explanation of certain philosophical or esoteric preoccupations. But if these symbolic representations had not been translations of familiar and recognizable ideas they would not have been resorted to so readily. Who would want to live in a house decorated with completely indecipherable symbols?

Even more commonplace were the practices intended to assure the victory of a favoured faction by the use of formulas supplied by sorcery or magic. The fanaticism of the races carried to such a pitch engendered superstition. This is not surprising. Astrologers who lived in the neighbourhood of the circus were consulted. They did not limit themselves to reading the results of the next race. They could procure for the partisan, or for his rival, those magical formulas which could call down a curse on a team or on its driver. It was enough to attach the leaden disc on which a curse was engraved to the neck of a dead man who thus acted as a post office for missives addressed to Hell, where the maleficent god for whom the message was intended lived.

In this field the astrologer could even provide a complete education; one charioteer, who was also a far-sighted parent, confided his son to a magician to be instructed in the art of sorcery and thus assure himself victory. Another anecdote, told by Ammianus Marcellinus, bears witness to the diffusion of these practices. A debtor, in order to rid himself of a too importunate creditor, brought an action accusing a charioteer of casting spells. The law, in fact, forbade sorcery, especially in this field. But the astrologers and magicians of all kinds who were from time to time expelled from the city with much uproar were never very long in returning. There was work to be done even in the palace of the emperor, who was intensely interested in receiving assurances about a future from which there was everything to fear. In such turbulent times, such a law was bound to remain a dead letter.

It would be tempting to see in this flowering of allegories and superstitions the reactions of a society on the eve of dissolution. And, in fact, the authors who have handed down to us the

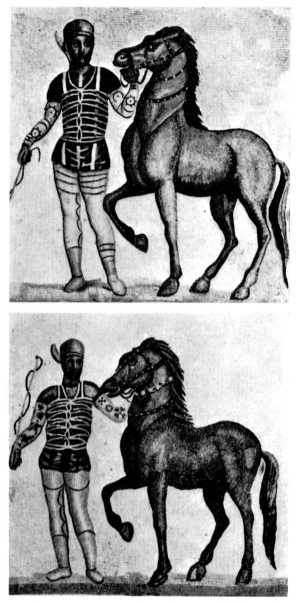

17. Charioteers wearing the colours of the 'factions'.
Mosaic in the National Museum, Rome. (Photo Alinari-
Giraudon)

18. Mosaic in the Barcelona Archaeological Museum, picturing the circus games. It shows in detail the decorations of the *spina*; to the right of Cybele, who is riding a lion, stands the obelisk, and next to it the structure supporting the 'eggs'; panthers, a victory, a temple. On her left is an altar, with symbols, Hercules with a club on his shoulder and lion's skin, the dolphins, oddly enough reduced to four in number. (Photo German Archaeological Institute, Madrid)

symbolism of the circus all wrote later than 500 A.D. But it is quite possible that they may all have used a lost book by Suetonius as a common source. Even if we do not go back as far as that, at least we know from the mosaics that at the beginning of the fourth century the symbolic interpretations of the institutions of the circus were a part of daily life.

Behind the scenes; the financial power of the factions

Behind the passions and the intrigues of all sorts there were economic realities which were doubtless in Roman eyes the most important aspect of the phenomenon; after all, is it the producer of a film or his stars which most interest the modern public?

The factions were business enterprises but not what we should call in our days direct producers. Save on rare occasions they did not organize spectacles for money-making ends. They provided the magistrates charged with giving the games with the equipment which they needed: chariots and horses, which were their property, and charioteers who were under contract to them. In its main lines, therefore, the system was similar to that which formerly controlled the gladiatorial combats, the factions playing the role of the *lanistas*.

But strangely enough, though from the first century onward the state had assured its own autonomy as regards the gladiatorial combats by creating menageries and barracks, whence it drew animals, gladiators and *bestiarii* necessary for these spectacles, it had abandoned to the private sector everything that concerned the circus. It is quite obvious that in the days of the Republic the magistrates were not in a position to maintain the studs and the personnel necessary to look after them. Something not unlike a craft organization was adequate for a troupe of gladiators: slaves, a few instructors and the outbuildings of a large country house sufficed. The investment needed for participation in the races involved quite different expenses, out of all proportion to those at the disposal of any individual. But the state?

We do not know exactly why it kept its hands off them.

K 145

Perhaps quite simply because, in one way or another, it drew sufficiently large revenues from the profits of the factions not to have had any interest in changing the system. Nero and Caligula increased the number of races to be given in a single day to the point where the number of chariots required was almost doubled. This was perhaps not due purely to a passion for sport or the desire for popularity. Commodus, for example, who also increased the number of races, was accused of wanting to enrich the faction directors. Pure philanthropy? We can hardly believe it when we recall that the treasury exercised a strict control on the factions, which, without the authorization of the emperor, could not accept gifts of horses or slaves to which the generosity of dignitaries attached to their colour prompted them. But this is guesswork.

At the head of these associations of owners formed in connection with the circus were the directors, the *domini factionum*, important personages who belonged to the equestrian order, as did almost everyone in the business world of Rome. They formed the *familia quadrigaria*, equivalent to the *familia gladiatoria*, employing a considerable number of men, put at about a hundred persons. This estimate has been disputed, but the numerical importance of these organizations becomes self-evident once one takes into account the list of employees of all sorts involved; besides the *doctores*, whose task was to train apprentices in the difficult art of keeping their footing on a chariot, there were charioteers and all the personnel needed to look after the horses. The associations also employed wheelwrights and shoemakers and even craftsmen who specialized in the making of ornaments intended for the horses, not to mention the administration required by an enterprise organized on such generous lines. We must take account also of the number of men needed to enter the lists, when twenty-four races were run in one day even if, as certain details suggest, each charioteer took part several times. So we must not be astonished to see a dignitary making a present of a batch of five slaves to his faction.

The studs included the most varied types of horses. If needs be, they were brought by sea, in specially designed ships similar to those used for the transport of cavalry, flat-bottomed lighters with a special framework which made them safer and more comfortable for the animals.

Nothing was allowed to stand in the way, when it was a question of getting hold of specially popular types; the Antioch studs, for example, did not hesitate to buy horses from Spain. It seems, moreover, that tastes varied from one city to another and from one period to another. Sicily, Africa, Thessaly, Cappadocia, disputed the honour of providing Rome with the best racers. These special breeds were also used for skilful cross-breeding and the resulting progeny subjected to a thorough training which lasted until the third year, when they began to take part in the races. But then the horses, of which the fanciers knew the pedigree and the number of wins, became real forms of wealth: the price of some of them was higher than that of an estate.

These details show the wealth of the factions, of which the really princely seat of the 'Blues' at Carthage has already given us an idea. They were real powers, which were sometimes linked financially with enterprises working in other branches of entertainment and therefore somewhat similar to our 'combines'. Their demands were as great as their means. Like the *lanistas* formerly, but on a different scale, since the chariot races recurred with great frequency in the programme of the games, the factions held an unassailable monopoly of names which nothing could replace in the affections of the public. Faced with this, of what avail was his fortune, more or less depleted by the extravagance of his forebears, to a wealthy man of note obliged in his capacity of magistrate to make a royal display?

He had to accept the schedule of charges presented to him, if he did not want to risk a dispute in which he could make himself ridiculous. There were, however, some who jibbed; in 54 the praetor Aulus Fabricius boldly attacked the financial tyranny of the factions by openly refusing to bow to their demands. An idea which he had doubtless been considering for a long time saved him; he replaced the horses by dogs. That must have made

147

a sensation, but the public would have certainly taken it ill had the jest been repeated. But only the 'Reds' and the 'Whites' gave way to this blackmail. The 'Blues' and the 'Greens', whose pre-eminence we have stressed many times, stuck to their guns. The emperor had to arbitrate in order to put an end to this conflict.

We know, moreover, what happened when a man took it into his head to circumvent the factions by using his own means to get hold of the equipment needed for the races. This is what Symmachus did, out of ambition, not meanness; he wanted the games given by his son to be especially magnificent and with this in view looked for something better than the *quadrigae* which Italy could offer. He sent experts to choose exceptional racehorses from the best studs in Spain and have them brought to Rome. To ease their task he called on all his acquaintances—of whom he had no lack—both private and official, from the Spanish authorities to landowners.

At the same time he sent to Sicily for charioteers who had doubtless acquired a reputation throughout the Empire. But he had no luck. They did not arrive. So he sent talent-scouts to the gulf of Salerno and at the same time organized, with the help of friends, a system of swift relays to Rome, and finally ordered the officials to make enquiries all along the coast to try to find the lost charioteers. Similar hazards had to be expected for the horses. Symmachus had therefore been compelled to assure himself of the co-operation of the Italian *quadrigae* in case of some irreparable accident and to ask a friend who lived in the region of Arles to put them up during the winter, should bad weather make navigation uncertain. Such were the worries from which on payment of a tidy sum the Roman factions freed a dignitary.

VI

THE REIGN OF THE STAR

The meaning of a famous episode

There are astonishing life-histories of which one should take note. That of Spartacus, whose epic story is known the world over, is not the only example. With eighty of his companions, armed only with spits and kitchen knives, he unexpectedly escaped from the gladiatorial school at Capua before the garrison had time to intervene. On his way he came across a providential arsenal, in the form of a convoy of carts taking weapons to the gladiators of some other town. The defeat of a local contingent, doubtless quite a strong one, provided him with an ample harvest of swords. In a symbolic gesture, they took them instead of the arms of the gladiators, regarded as dishonourable and barbarian, which they had used until then. These were used for arming the slaves who came from all sides to swell the ranks of the victor's small troupe.

Cohorts ordered to suppress the revolt then set out from Rome, under the command of praetors and later of consuls. Spartacus' strength lay in the spirit that inspired his band. For all that the facts gave them the lie, the Romans, whether leaders or soldiers, could not bring themselves to look upon this punitive expedition as a war or to consider as enemies those whom their prejudices led them to lump together as a worthless rabble. The Romans were ignominiously routed several times; and Spartacus, making the conqueror abide by his own customs, forced the Roman prisoners to fight as gladiators over the tombs of his officers. He was filled with the despairing energy which men

149

can display in battle when defeat is the only alternative to ignoble punishment.

But he was weakened by that irresolution, so well described by Flaubert when writing of the mercenaries of Carthage, which is inevitably displayed by this sort of army once the imperious demands of a definite action no longer hold it together, and which is a consequence of the situation itself. Vacillation between the lust for an immediate vengeance and the more prudent project of regaining one's own country, the exaltation of victory and the confused realization of the weakness which results from the absence of sound organization in a struggle against an organized state, engender over-confidence, uncertainty and dissension. The exploit, after prodigies of courage and ingenuity into which we shall not go, ended in defeat. Yet it had been necessary, after the praetors and the consuls, to send Crassus against 'a deserter, a gladiator and a brigand' and even to recall Pompey the Great from Spain.

Such a fate, in the days when the spectacles had reached the degree of organization which we have described, was inconceivable. The personality of Spartacus could only have emerged within definite historical limits. There were, under the Empire, a few rare attempts at revolt in the gladiatorial schools, notably at Praeneste. But the Romans escaped at the cost of a panic which Tacitus reports in disdainful terms: the revolts miscarried. Experience had given rise to precautions against this sort of attempt by means of Draconian measures which doomed them to defeat from the start. Supervision was so well organized in the schools that the Romans were not afraid to install them in the very centre of the city; the control of practice arms was strict and guards were ready to intervene at the slightest incident. It would moreover not have been easy, at this time, to transform any insurrection into a civil war.

There was no longer any escape from this universe by breaching the walls, but only by professional success. This could take the form of the image of Épinal, a sort of semi-deification, or the cruder form of a prince's favour. In the more commonplace social register it conferred or seemed to confer on the life of these men, charioteers, gladiators, *venatores*, almost all of base extraction, a brilliance and glamour which could satisfy a vague feeling for the marvellous. In actual fact the inconceivable could happen in this domain. One day the mother of Hierocles, who was working as a slave in the heart of Caria, saw soldiers coming towards her; they escorted her with great pomp to Rome, where she was installed among the wives of former consuls; her son, a charioteer, had attracted the attention of the emperor and, to all intents and purposes, governed in his place. Asiaticus was a freedman whom Vitellius (who, according to Suetonius, 'governed most of the time on the advice and according to the desires of the basest of actors or charioteers') had made his favourite. But the young man wearied of this intimacy and preferred to make his living in a provincial town selling rough wine; he was recaptured and put into irons. Shortly after, Vitellius pardoned him, but soon regretted his weakness. Exasperated by the independence and thievishness of Asiaticus, he sold him to an itinerant *lanista*. The former favourite thus found himself helmeted. But as luck, or the circumspection of the *lanista*, had reserved him for the last combat, Vitellius had him taken out of the arena 'all of a sudden'. Let us leave this eventful story at this point, since we shall have to treat elsewhere of the precise role played by such men in society. A detail taken from Dio Cassius will be enough accurately to define the atmosphere of this sort of life history. He says, speaking of Hierocles, that 'noticed by the prince, he was immediately taken from the circus and brought to the palace'. These reverses of fortune, identical to those of the heroes of Petronius, became the more frequent the more free men began to seek in such careers a remedy for their disappointed hopes.

Paradoxically, the most terrible of these professions, that of the gladiator, ended by becoming a 'way out' for the improvident. A whimsical anecdote perfectly illustrates this state of mind: two friends who had come to Greece to study, Toxaris and Sisinnes, were robbed in an inn, and found themselves totally without resources. Some gladiators whom they met on the way to the amphitheatre having told them that 'they lacked nothing', Sisinnes made up his mind to free his friend from his embarrassment and at the same time to make him rich. As the spectacle was about to begin, and a herald, according to a procedure similar to an auction, conceivable perhaps in some small provincial town or simply invented by Lucian, produced a tall young man and asked who was ready to confront him, Sisinnes advanced into the middle of the arena, received the reward of 10,000 drachmas and handed them to his friend. Such a story, which evokes by its sentimentality ar 1 its improbabilities our 'bourgeois dramas' of the eighteenth century, served as the background for a speech by Quintilian.

These moralizing themes betray the existence of a compensatory myth, which gratified a society for which disdain for human life was an accepted institution. At first it treated the actor or the protagonist as a thing. Under the Empire the change in manners and customs had greatly attenuated the harshness of this attitude and, for all that something of it survived, had modified the material conditions of the 'actors' and their social status, which became henceforth ambiguous, since it belonged partly to the old tradition and partly to the new psychology, which were very often diametrically opposed to each other.

But first let us see whence these men came.

The road to the barracks

For the simple reason that there was always a stigma of infamy attached to these professions, the men who took them up were, with a very few exceptions, drawn from the most disinherited classes of society. There were, none the less, nuances in the scorn in which they were held. The charioteers were distinguished from the gladiators and the *bestiarii* in that their profession did not, in itself, imply any legal degradation. Already in the times of the Republic young men gloried in their prowess in handling a chariot. They could be seen, regardless of the bystanders, filling the streets with the deafening clatter of their wheels. It even seems that at a certain period it was not regarded as shocking for respectable men to drive their own chariots. This practice did not become universal, but this sport never lost its aristocratic tinge, which doubtless had something to do with its popularity. This is enough to explain why no special stigma attached to the profession of charioteer, even though many of them were slaves or came from the faceless mass of non-citizens which swarmed in the slums of Rome.

It was by no means the same with the gladiators and the *bestiarii*, objects of a scorn to which we shall soon refer, and whose recruitment, for this among other reasons, was subject to all sorts of legal restrictions. The first gladiators, we recall, were prisoners to whom swords were given.

The custom of making them fight at funerals quickly disappeared, but the method of recruitment remained the same. After a victorious campaign or the suppression of a revolt, the generals and especially the emperors found thousands of prisoners at their disposal. This human mass was then sorted out; some were sold as slaves or employed as such by the state, others were thrown to the beasts or massacred in the amphitheatres of the Empire. But the strongest among them were reserved for the gladiatorial schools, the *ludi*, which, in the circumstances, was not the worst of fates. This, for example, happened to the Jewish prisoners, some of whom were massacred in the games given at Caesarea, while a contingent was reserved for the construction of the Colosseum, and the remainder distributed among the gladiatorial schools of Greece. These massive contributions, which were repeated under several emperors, were clearly insufficient to provide for the vast reserves of men which the development of this type of spectacle required.

Who, then, became a gladiator? Men who, juridically speaking, had no choice: criminals and slaves. But there were also, from the very first days of the Empire, free men. The slaves formed the social class that provided by far the greatest number of gladiators. They were sometimes sent to the school as a punishment, for the crime of flight, for example, though that was unusual. Owing to their very condition they were liable without let or sanction to be sent there at the will of their master. He had the right of selling them, or hiring them or of exploiting them in the amphitheatre without being subjected to any special legal formality, in the same way as he could put a female slave to work as a prostitute. On the other hand, a slave was not permitted to escape the cruelty of a master or a dreaded punishment by enrolling as a gladiator, a principle which aggravated the inhumanity of the system but which was the inevitable consequence of the absolute property rights of the master. The emperors, in their desire to prevent a slave from avoiding a punishment at his master's hands by choosing this last resource, caused it to be observed with the utmost strictness. This legislation remained in force up to the time of Hadrian, when it seems that it was modified; thenceforward, in order to force a slave to become a gladiator, it was necessary either to get his consent or to show proof of an offence which made him liable to the *damnatio ad ludum*.

On this particular point, therefore, there was henceforth no essential difference between the slave and the free man; only those sentenced or those enrolled became gladiators. The *damnatio ad ludum*, in fact, was a penalty *sui generis*, similar to the death penalty or forced labour in the mines but, generally speaking, less severe than the latter. However, it must not be confused with sentence to death by the sword in the amphitheatre on the occasion of the midday games which, like the condemnation *ad bestias*, was an aggravation of the death penalty; in the latter case, as we have seen, neither luck nor the clemency of the spectators could save a man deprived of all means of defence; in the former case a man was sent to the *ludus*, where he received a training in every way similar to that of the other novices. The risk he ran of death in the amphitheatre was therefore governed by the rules of his profession and his chances of survival depended upon his bravery and his skill. Nor was it a question of a life sentence; if luck enabled him to survive the combats in which he took part, after three years he no longer had to appear in the arena; he ended his term in the *ludus*, where for another two years he carried out some duty or other. None the less, this punishment was a pretty severe penalty for a free man. For, apart from the risk of death and the infamy which it implied, it also meant years of extremely hard life in which the most drastic punishments were the rule. It was in this way that serious crimes, such as sacrilege, arson or military disobedience, when it reached the proportions of mutiny, were punished.

It is, moreover, possible that there was sometimes a tendency to add to the list of these crimes, since the sentences afforded an easy way of filling the gladiatorial barracks. But the abuses committed by certain emperors are not a sure proof. We know that the less scrupulous among them did not hesitate to force peaceable citizens to fight in the arena, 'either individually', as Dio Cassius writes, 'or in a body as in a pitched battle'. Caligula one day even asked the authorization of the Senate to do so— pure derision, as the same historian remarks, since he could put to death no matter whom just as he pleased.

In reality, it does not seem that the men so taken were ever sent to the *ludus*. They were purely and simply thrown into the arena, sword in hand, as is proved by a passage from Suetonius, who says that one day Claudius made one of his heralds, dressed as he was (that is to say in a toga), go down into the arena. These were therefore real death sentences; can we picture a peaceable official in this state standing up to the assaults of a trained brute? Such an abuse, it is true, was in all probability one among many and it could well be that men were sent to the *ludus* quite arbitrarily and for mere peccadilloes. Everything was possible under emperors who, like Caligula, on the pretext that there was a shortage of meat for the beasts, were capable of throwing to them as food all the inmates of a prison, without distinction.

Voluntary enrolments

Ordinarily, the emperors who, from the end of the first century

155

A.D., were the most important owners of *ludi* could also count on voluntary enrolments to replenish their ranks. It is a fact that under the Empire such enrolments became everyday occurrences, and not only among the lower classes; knights and senators appeared in the arena, men who, in Juvenal's phrase, 'were more noble than the Capitolini, than the Marcelli . . ., than all the spectators seated on the *podium* not excepting even the very man who gave the games'—in this particular case, Nero. In the time of Augustus this was still unusual; but soon no more notice was paid to it, the phenomenon having become commonplace, despite the many laws enacted to curb this degradation, which was considered shameful.

The free man who enrolled faced not only the dangers of the combats but also the harshness of a convict's life. Though theoretically still free, or rather regaining his status as a free man at the end of his engagement, he lowered himself for the time being to the rank of a slave. He became the chattel of a master and of his own accord fell into the legal category of the *infames*, that is to say the pariahs. He received, symbolically, even before being recognized as a gladiator, the punishment reserved for slaves, the rods. In the eyes of the Romans, that was such a degradation that up to the end of the Republic it was inconceivable that an honourable man should expose himself to it. Later, it is true, their outlook changed in this respect. Men grew accustomed to seeing Nero daily seeking for success on the stage. Caligula spent his time either as a charioteer or as a Thracian gladiator. With Commodus the need to show himself in the arena was an obsession. As Juvenal said: when the prince is a lyre player it is not surprising that a noble should become an actor. But a gladiator? As we shall soon see, the feelings of the public about everything connected with the life of a gladiator were ambivalent; but undoubtedly there was always considerable scorn for a man who thus debased himself to the level of a slave.

It is clear that a taste for danger and the attraction of arms sometimes decided a man to ignore this. One such man, of noble origin, justified himself on his epitaph for having embraced this profession with the words: 'Everyone takes his pleasure where he finds it. . . .' The knights, of whom Dio Cassius writes, declared that they considered the infamy attached to this profession as of no account. But they were the exceptions. The rest were driven purely and simply by the need for money. Juvenal, on several occasions, and Seneca speak of these irresponsible nobles for whom ruin and enrolment lay in wait. They spent without counting the price; luxury was for them of no value unless it bore the stamp of originality. Their table was a festival. To satiate a gluttony which had taken on the proportions of a vice they first pledged their tableware or 'broke in pieces the bust of their mother'. Yet each gigantic turbot, each delicacy, brought them nearer to the gladiator's bowl; and one fine day, amid universal derision, they went to find the tribune, happy enough to be able to get food and a resting-place by selling their bodies. In short, they remained the slaves of their bellies to the end.

There is doubtless a good deal of rhetoric in this manner of presenting the facts and a moralizing tendency is evident. For what could a man hope for, in such circumstances, by becoming a gladiator? There was a bonus on enrolment, but it was not more than 2,000 sesterces. It was a derisory sum when a single one of these extraordinary delicacies which had ruined the new recruit could cost up to 400 sesterces. Furthermore, food and a roof were assured him, but at such a price that any other solution would have been preferable. In reality, what decided these ruined men to opt for this was not so much slavery to the belly, which was common enough, as the hope, or the illusion, befitting this sort of temperament, of being able rapidly to recoup the squandered fortune by means of the rewards of an unusual career. That said, there is no question but that pure and simple penury must have forced a good many wretches to accept this solution in a moment of weakness or thoughtlessness; and that was the true reason for the majority of enrolments.

To take this irrevocable step, the future recruits were if necessary given encouragements of questionable value. Naturally, the greatest interest was shown in young and sturdy men capable of becoming good gladiators, whose disorderly life gave an opportunity for blackmail. Gold, produced at a suitable moment, was used, as well as promises and threats. This was the custom not only in Rome but in small *municipia*, where the wiles of the crimps were particularly successful among the simple. The law, however, afforded the free man guarantees which should, in principle, have forestalled these 'impulsive acts' and controlled the frauds; he could not enrol without having made a preliminary declaration before a tribune of the plebs, without which the contract made with the proprietor of the *ludus* would have been invalid. But, following the great increase in enrolments, this declaration fairly soon lost the solemn and protective character which it was intended to have and became a simple formality.

When the recruits, drawn from all countries, from the banks of the Nile to those of the Danube, and from all levels of society, had taken the customary oath, the *ludus* received them in rows of cells, some without sky-lights, which lined the square where they exercised. It was a prison, or at least the most forbidding of barracks. At Pompeii, the cells ranged on two levels, were four yards long and without means of inter-communication. An immense kitchen, the far wall of which had a kitchen-range along its whole length, occupied the centre of one of the sides of the rectangle; there was a prison, in the exact sense of the term, and an armoury. The yard was bare, but surrounded by columns whose flutings and red designs gave a surprising note of gaiety to this sinister spot. Their embellishments, if not their existence, are admittedly explained by the fact that the yard had formerly been the portico of the Great Theatre, later transformed into a *ludus*.

The favoured site for these barracks may have changed; at one time Capua had a monopoly of them. It was a city of gladiators, like our own garrison towns. Under the Empire *ludi* were not only to be found in Rome but also in the most distant provinces, at Pergamon or Alexandria. So too their owners; depending on the period for the most part a professional trader (*lanista*), an aristocrat or the emperor. That, it seems, in no way affected the physical organization of the *ludus*; one built by Domitian has the same plan as the one at Pompeii. It was the proportions that changed. Instead of from 150 to 200 gladiators, the *ludus* had 1,000 or more.

The personnel of the *ludi*, as we have said, was known as the *familia gladiatoria*. This term, which was originally applied to a household staff of slaves, betrays the craft origins of the institution. But we must not be misled by the associations of the modern equivalent of this word. On his arrival the future gladiator was enrolled with the most terrible of oaths. In the prison of the *ludus* of Pompeii have been found some of the fetters which prevented the prisoner from standing upright. But the treatment implied by this sort of instrument was not the worst to which a gladiator had to submit. He swore also to endure the whip, the branding iron and death by the sword. The inhumanity of this discipline was excused not only by the need to bring hardened criminals to heel and to tame the 'hot-heads' among the recruits. It was intended, above all, to nip in the bud any tendency to rebellion which was bound to arise once some of these men became aware of the fact that the harshness and injustice of the life they were to lead were beyond anything they had imagined. Only fear of the most terrible punishments could produce that moral conditioning of which we have seen examples in the arena, inculcating in the gladiators, until it became a reflex, that determination to surmount every kind of test which was their one hope of salvation. Two Thracians whom Caligula maintained in his miniature *ludus* at Rome are cited as models; threatened with no matter what, they would not even blink.

The making of future champions

One can imagine how systematic and rigorous a training was required to get to this pitch. In one sense the gladiators, like the charioteers and the *bestiarii*, were technicians who, in this world where men were sold, could like any other 'specialized' slave, such as a doctor or a tutor, represent a real capital asset. It took years to train a good gladiator, for over-indulgence in the spectacles had made the public exacting.

The first steps were made under the direction of the *doctores*, masters of swordsmanship who specialized in the use of different weapons; there was a *doctor secutorum*, a *doctor thracicum*, etc. There was even a *doctor* for the very special arms of the *sagittarii*. In order to improve the quality of his gladiatorial team, Caesar had had the idea of entrusting their training to senators and knights famous for their knowledge of swordsmanship. But usually the *doctores* were former gladiators, whom perfect mastery of their art had allowed to grow old.

In the rectangular yard of the school their curt orders (*dictata*) punctuated the complicated gymnastics of men engaging a stationary adversary, a stake fixed in the ground (*palus*), two yards high, heavily marked by blows. The swordplay was essentially that prescribed for the combats; the footwork, the attack alternately with sword and buckler thrust forward. These exercises were not carried out with actual weapons, but with the *rudis*, a wooden sword reserved for training, and a wicker buckler. Naturally, the exercises were not the same for all; the *doctor* taught the veterans the subtleties which he had learnt during a whole lifetime in the profession. It seems, in fact, according to Louis Robert, that the term *palus*, which originally meant the training post, ended by being applied to squads into which the gladiators were divided according to their degree of skill; there were supposedly four of them, called respectively *primus palus*, *secundus palus*, etc.

It is moreover certain that these basic exercises at the stake did not exclude other forms of training, including duels with naked weapons; otherwise it would be hard to understand the care taken to create in the Roman *ludus* an exact replica of the arena in the form of a walled ellipse, the same size as the one in which the gladiator would have to manoeuvre on the day of combat. On the other hand, for certain exercises they used real weapons heavier than the normal ones. The combats were as much a test of endurance as of skill and this precaution ensured

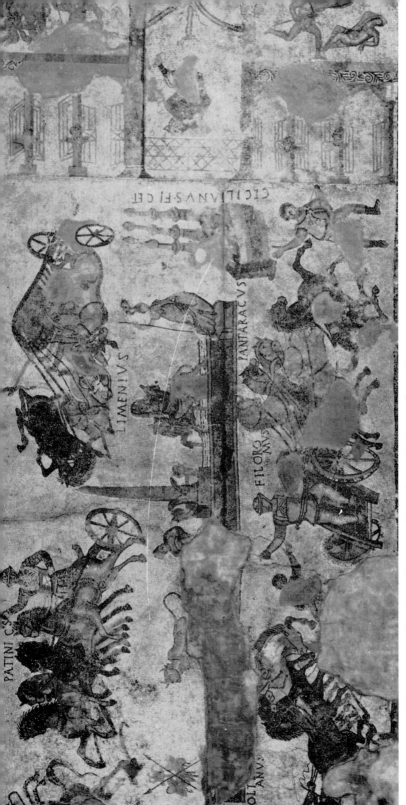

19. Mosaic in the Barcelona Museum. One of the charioteers has 'shipwrecked' and is entangled in his harness. (Photo German Archaeological Institute, Madrid)

20(a) The Emperor of Byzantium, surrounded by his family and cour presents the victor's crown. The solemnity of the ceremony bears witnes to the importance of the circus in the life of the city. Plinth of the obelis of Theodosius at Istanbul. (Photo Boudot-Lamotte)

20(b) The amphitheatre at Capua. It was here that the revolt led by Spartacu began. (Photo Boudot-Lamotte)

that the gladiator's strength should not betray him inopportunely. He had to be able 'to endure, all day long, in the full sun, in the scorching dust, dripping with blood . . .'. A few months of training were clearly not enough to bring the novice to such a point. But at least they enabled him to confront an adversary in his own class and to make an honourable showing. After this first combat he was no longer a *tiro*; he was well on the way to becoming a veteran and then began the real dangers.

We could repeat, almost word for word, what has been said about the gladiators in describing the *venatores*, the specialists in fighting wild beasts. It will be recalled that barbarian tribes were at first often called on for the purpose, such as had perfected hunting techniques, as the Getuli against elephants. But the success and frequency of this type of spectacle made it necessary to create a specialized staff; there was, therefore, at Rome from the time of Domitian a *ludus matutinus* (a term explicable by the fact that the 'hunts' took place in the morning), corresponding exactly to the *ludus magnus* of the gladiators. Recruitment was, for the most part, similar; slaves, criminals, men under contract— it is said of these last that they sometimes had difficulty in choosing between the two—and so was the specialization; there were *succursores*, *taurarii*, *sagittarii*, etc. Barbarians, however, continued to act as instructors; a man learnt the handling of the bow from Parthians, that of the lance from Moors. All in all, the conditions of life and of work were similar; but the profession of *venator* was considered even more infamous than that of gladiator.

It was no easier to learn to drive a chariot than to become a master swordsman. Despite the paucity of our information on this subject, we know that it usually took several years of practice before an apprentice was equal to facing competition. He had to learn not only to drive, but also how to fall. It was no easy matter when crouching to manage to cut the reins wound round his waist at the moment when the chariot began to crack under him. The vicissitudes of the profession, moreover, were not limited to the danger of death, real enough as the inscriptions bear witness; the charioteer could also emerge crippled or maimed

L

by the brutal falls, in which he could easily break his bones on the wreckage of the chariot, assuming he was not dragged along by his team. The needed reflexes and all the tricks of the trade were acquired under the direction of *doctores* within the framework of the *familia quadrigaria* which was made up of a considerable staff working to provide all the needs of man and beast.

Doubtless great tenacity was needed to enable a man to stand out from the crowd. We are reminded of those Spanish urchins who are to be seen on waste ground handling an imaginary *muleta* with a schoolmate playing the bull, repeating the same pass time and time again and who, grown older, go at night to practice among the reserves of young bulls, at risk of a gunshot. But, if he were not mown down in the flower of his youth, our man could, like that charioteer of Carthage, build himself a comfortable villa on a height overlooking the circus when he retired, within sight of the place, the presence of which had become for him a physical need.

The conquest of glory

'Hermes', says Martial, speaking of a gladiator, 'is the toast of Rome and of his century. Hermes is skilled in the use of all weapons. Hermes is a gladiator and a master of swordsmanship; Hermes strikes fear and terror into his opponents. Hermes knows how to win and to win without a blow. There is no one to replace him, except himself.' Like the *bestiarius* Carpophorus or the charioteer Scorpus, he was, in fact, what we should today call a star.

In fact the popularity enjoyed by such men was comparable to that enjoyed by our own celebrities. Their names had that magic quality that arouses passion. The crowd applauded them even before they appeared and clamoured for them, yelling and shouting; often, at the end of an afternoon, the insatiable spectators filling the amphitheatre, carried away by the excitement of a spectacle, chanted the sonorous names of those gladiators who were the glory and adornment of their *ludus*: Triumphus, Spiculus, Rutuba, Tetraides. . . . It then behoved the liberality of the emperor to ensure that they appeared, for their persons were worth a fortune. Not content with receiving the ovations that, on their victorious evenings, resounded as far as the Roman Campagna, the charioteers also had their statues: the 'shiny nose of Scorpus' was seen everywhere in the city. The fact that they were mostly of servile origin conferred on that honour, commonplace enough but needless to say reserved for the well-to-do, the value of a real privilege. They gathered round them a regular court which accompanied them everywhere and their passing through the street was an event which excited more commotion than the appearance of some exalted personage. The very horses were the objects of a Hollywood-style adoration—the 'Bird', for example, of which Lucius Verus always wore a golden effigy rather like a fetish, and which he treated with a refinement worthy of the most temperamental film star: fed on raisins and dates and decked with purple, this horse, later buried on the Vatican hill, had the run of the palace.

To these spontaneous or delirious tributes, the poets added a nobler glory by celebrating the exploits of these champions in their verses. Martial, for example was not too proud to write three panegyrics of the *bestiarius* Carpophorus in his *Liber spectaculorum*, and so insistent and fulsome are his praises that one can only suppose that he must have been a favourite of Domitian who, as is well known, was very fond of this form of sport. This man of exceptional strength and cunning, whose youth the poet stresses, is ranked among the demi-gods; the glory of Meleager or Hercules is but a pale shadow of his. He outstrips the lion in speed and destroys it, he overcomes the bear with a blow of his spear, he can bring down a score of ferocious beasts in a single day and yet leave the arena alert and fresh. Had he been born in legendary times when monsters abounded he could have rid the world of them unaided. . . . This dithyramb is no exception. The same poet could reserve the best of his verbal acrobatics for the charioteer Scorpus, who died at the age of twenty-seven at the height of his success and whose wealth and popularity he celebrates elsewhere: 'O heinous crime.

You die, Scorpus, in the flower of your youth and go so soon to harness the raven steeds of Hell! Why do you pass the boundaries of life as quickly as your chariot passed the boundary marks of the circus?' And later: 'The jealous Fates that carried me off at twenty-seven thought, on counting my victories, that I was already old.'

To that was often added the open favour of the emperor or of high dignitaries. That of the former was not constant, but it was limitless when shown. It was above all shown to charioteers, whom the emperor visited, invited to his orgies and reckoned among his personal friends, when that is one of them did not find himself officially promoted to the rank of favourite.

It was thus that Caligula, who assiduously frequented the stable of the 'Green' faction, to the extent of taking his meals there, conceived a lasting friendship for Eutyches. It drove him so far—and this act was suicidal—as to demand that the Praetorians undertook a task dishonourable to them, that of erecting stables for his favourite's horses. As for Hierocles, the favourite of Elagabalus, he really and truly governed and, according to Dio Cassius, enjoyed an authority greater even than that of the emperor himself. After these, one dare not mention the more modest dignities to which even gladiators attained, such as commander of the imperial guard, or the privilege, enjoyed by the whole guild of charioteers, of being able, without risk of legal action, to indulge in 'pranks' in the manner of students in former days, including theft and the beating-up of passers-by.

Glory brought also more tangible benefits. Money, to an extent, however, difficult to assess, followed fame. The gladiator whom several years of combat had turned into a skilled man received a sum six times larger than the ordinary enrolment bonus as his re-engagement fee. But to this legally fixed amount due to him, the *lanista* added an additional sum which varied according to the favour in which the man was held by the public. Furthermore, the value of the rewards traditionally given to the victor depended on the qualities he had displayed; thus it happened that in some interminable combat in which two famous gladiators were pitted against each other, the emperor repeatedly gave each of them presents, becoming more liberal the longer the fight went on, to compensate for the refusal of the *missio,* loudly demanded by the populace.

In this matter also the charioteers were the most favoured. They received not only the rewards which they had the right to claim from the spectators after victory but also money from the factions, which did not exclusively command their allegiance, but fought one another for it. On several occasions, moreover, it was found necessary to fix a maximum remuneration for both charioteers and gladiators, but to very little effect. It was scarcely to be expected that people would keep to this when they said that it did not prevent the emperors from privately making the most extravagant gifts. The very fact of forming part of the emperor's circle and of sharing his table was the source of untold wealth; the gladiator Spiculus received inheritances and houses from Nero, and Eutyches, of whom we spoke earlier, two million sesterces from Caligula. These were exceptional cases, but even so many possessed a fortune and could, for example, afford the luxury of freeing a slave in order to celebrate a victory. So much so that for the poets, who were reduced to soliciting meagre pensions by means of flattery, the charioteers, whose wealth Juvenal reckons as equal to that of a hundred or more lawyers, could pass as symbols of wealth. There were even some who, once employees and now masters, became partners in the faction trusts.

And yet, for some of these men at least, success brought with it a benefit of considerably more value than fees. It is incomprehensible to us that a man could simultaneously rouse the enthusiasm of the crowd and yet not be firmly in possession of any rights other than those of a pack-animal exposed to all the whims of a workhouse beadle. To the paradox of stars in barracks, true at least so far as the gladiators were concerned, must be added another of much greater generality: the majority of 'actors' of all kinds were deprived of that blessing enjoyed by even the most disinherited of the streets—liberty. They had no choice, so far as their future was concerned, but to acquiesce; their children were slaves by birth, on the same level as the meanest labourer; if, for example, they were taken in adultery *in flagrante delicto* they were liable to the death penalty, without any form of trial.

Now, if the favour of the prince provided affluence and luxury, that of the people conferred liberty, a reward not so easy to obtain as one might think, for the more popular a gladiator, a *bestiarius* or a charioteer, the more would his emancipation involve his owner in an appreciable loss. Only the insistence of the people could force him to accept it. In such a case it was usually the emperor who made the decision, even for men who did not belong to him. But the displeasure which Tiberius one day manifested at having to give way in such a case, when one of his own actors was in question, proves that the enthusiasm of the crowd could force the hand even of the most reluctant emperor. Certain emperors tried to guard against this by passing a law declaring emancipations obtained in this way null and void, and Hadrian one day refused to accede, in terms which clearly stressed that in the circumstances the people were showing themselves generous on the cheap. 'It is not for you,' he said to the onlookers, 'to ask me to emancipate a slave belonging to another.' It seems, however, that despite the hazards to which it was subjected, the obtaining of liberty must have become a regular thing, in the long or the short term, for those gladiators or charioteers who had long since made their mark.

The story of Eppia

To the favour of the court and the people was added that of the women which the very general relaxation of morals sometimes transformed into passion. It must be said, however, that neither gladiators nor charioteers had pride of place in this matter. Tragedy, a dying art, had given place to a very special type of 'pantomime' in which specialized actors, using only gesture and mime, 'played' dramatic episodes from the lives of the heroes and the gods. Everything in this art, therefore, depended on suggestion. The subjects dealt particularly with the scabrous adventures which the Greeks attributed to the inhabitants of Olympus. It may be imagined to what degree of erotic intensity refinement of gesture could bring this mute and subtle evocation of the loves of Jupiter or of Venus. A passage from Juvenal clearly suggests the avidity of the glances, the tense silence, peculiar to this type of representation:

'Look around the arcades, try to pick out a woman who's worthy of your devotion. Check every tier of seats at all the theatres in town: will they yield one single candidate you could love without a qualm? When the effeminate Bathyllus lasciviously dances Leda, just watch the women. Tuccia can't control herself, Apula suddenly moans in drawn-out ecstasy, as though at the climax of passion. Thymele's all rapt attention, she's learning fast.'

Owing to this mixture of refinement and sensuality, which distinguished the pantomime from the Atellan plays, crude farces studded with obscene jokes and gestures, it was a form of theatre calculated to appeal to a surfeited aristocracy. The actors, all remarkable for their perfect beauty, became the objects of infatuations that gave rise to endless gossip in the fashionable world. The greatest ladies, including the wives of the emperors, argued about them, and the passion of Messalina for Mnester and of Domitia for Paris are still famous. The success of these actors was such that they were invited to private houses and on certain days the whole city resounded with the noise of dances in which they were the leaders.

The passion for gladiators, less general but not unusual, was the concomitant of excesses of a more animal sensuality, unless indeed one would prefer to call it the height of refinement. For those who gave way to it were not modest young girls naively moved by the prestige of a helmet, but mature and wealthy matrons whose perversions were aroused by the sight of scars. Recalling the story of Eppia, Juvenal does not fail to stress that she was the wife of a senator and that in her babyhood she had slept 'surrounded by her father's wealth, on swansdown, in a cradle trimmed with gold'. Was it because he was beautiful that Eppia followed Sergiolus? The portrait of the chosen gladiator makes it doubtful; he was no longer young and probably his beard, which he had begun to shave as he came nearer to retirement, was sprinkled with white hairs, fore-runners of old age. An 'acrid humour' dripped continually from one of his eyes; his nose, deformed by the helmet, had a large bump in the middle. A face which, all in all, smelt of misery and threatened ruin.

For such a man Eppia was able to endure every humiliation and to face the discomfort of a harsh life. The school to which Sergiolus belonged was that of an itinerant *lanista* who knocked about from one province to another, as far as Asia Minor and Egypt. It was thus not enough to be nomadic; one also needed sailors' legs. This fact furnished the poet with a cutting parallel:

'To go aboard ship is torture under a husband's orders: then the smell of the bilges is sickening, then the sky wheels dizzily around. But a wife who's off with her lover suffers no qualms. The one vomits over her husband, the other sits down to a hearty meal with the crew, takes a turn on the quarter-deck, helps to haul on the sheets, and enjoys it.'

The excitement of adventure must have made her oblivious of scorn and dishonour. Everywhere Eppia became known as the 'Gladiatrix'. To appreciate the force of this insult it must be remembered that some old-fashioned moral prejudices were still fairly widespread according to which the gladiator was even lower than the slave. One finds in Latin authors especially a curious insistence on the foul and repugnant nature of the gladiators' food, which did not, however, differ in any way from that of the soldiers. But this 'skilly', this 'mess-tin' into which ready-cooked scraps were thrown pell-mell, was foul, because it represented the price paid for the purchase of marketable blood: more unworthy still than the man who had 'rented his voice' was the gladiator who had sold his body, who was no more than a walking corpse fattened as geese are fattened. He had, to use Seneca's expression, '*to give back to the arena* what he eats and what he drinks'. Thus it was for a man of this stamp that Eppia abandoned her husband and her children and, by going far from Rome, everything else that she loved most—the plays of the pantomime artist Paris and the chariot races. The secret was simple: 'He was a gladiator.'

Graffiti found on the walls of the barracks at Pompeii—one of the inmates of which was called *suspirium puellarum* ('heart-throb') and *decus puellarum*—attest to the likelihood of the anecdote and we shall soon be examining another, this time a historical one.

But the fascination exercised by the champions of the arena did not lead all women to such excesses. Some of them were content very discreetly to pass an hour or two every day at the *ludus* among their favourites. There they put on the helmet and the greaves and had a go at the *palus* (stake) with the excited ardour of the neophyte, careful not to overlook a single piece of advice given them by their fencing-master and proud, once the exercise was over, to throw over their shoulders the Tyrian mantle prescribed in such circumstances before going to lie down for the traditional massage.

We know, though without further details, that women some-times fought in the arena. But for the most part attendance at the *ludus* did not imply any professional ambition. It was simply one of the most daring and original forms of snobbery. These 'gladiatrices', moreover, did not need to make an exhibition of themselves in front of the whole city for the licence in which they indulged to be regarded as the very acme of moral aberration by some few Romans imbued with respect for tradition. For these there was something about this usurpation so utterly contrary to established order that made it virtually a sacrilege. In this respect the manner in which Juvenal condemns Eppia is quite characteristic if only one takes the trouble to read between the lines; the most serious fault of this woman was not to love a

169

man to the point of immodesty or to degrade herself socially by shameful choice; her vice really consisted in 'loving the sword'. It was the sword that fascinated her and this indecorous fetishism, in which lay her perversion, turned Eppia into someone quite distinct from those merely sensual, shameless or pleasure-seeking women listed in the course of the same satire—and also more immoral. Stirred to the depths of her being by the same unnatural passion as the 'gladiatrices' of whom we have just been speaking, she merely chose to indulge her passion in another manner.

Emperor-charioteers

Complementing the aberration which we have just described was the no less astonishing brood of emperors who made exhibition of themselves in the games of the arena or the circus. Nothing better illustrates the prestige enjoyed by charioteers, gladiators and *bestiarii* than the ardour and persistence with which certain emperors laboured to imitate them. Today we can hardly conceive of our leaders, whatever their taste for sport, jumping onto the gleaming cycles of the Tour de France. In Rome this sort of vagary was sufficiently common not to be classed among the follies of a few mentally deranged men. With some, this insensate desire to ape the stars of the arena betrayed no more than the passion of the devotee; so it was with Didius Julianus, who came to it only in later life, or with Lucius Verus who, sent to the East to direct the war against the Parthians, devoted the better part of his time to training as a gladiator and a *bestiarius* without budging from Antioch. It was Marcus Aurelius who, from Rome where he had remained, directed the course of the campaign. Sometimes it took the form of a grotesque braggadocio. Nero decided to fight and overcome a lion in the arena, and a whole specialized staff 'prepared' the animal in order to reduce it to such a state of prostration that it became harmless.

But most often it reached the pitch of maniacal obsession such as made madmen of Nero, Caligula and, above all, Commodus, who had, so to speak, transformed his palace into an arena. He practised killing beasts there, as other men play chess. He also fought against gladiators, caring nothing about shedding blood in his own home. That did not prevent him from appearing frequently in public, something which, despite precedents, meant going one step further in setting aside convention. Shame prevented him only from driving a chariot in public 'except perhaps', as Dio Cassius says, 'on moonless nights, held back as he was, despite his desire to practise this art in the sight of all, by the shame of being seen taking part in it'. He made up for this discretion, it is true, by the unparalleled setting displayed when he fought in the arena as a gladiator or a *bestiarius*. On his arrival he ceremonially exchanged his sumptuous garments for a simple tunic. From the moment of his first 'victories' carefully orchestrated plaudits burst from the *podium* where the senators were seated and from the tiers occupied by the knights. On some days they were given the words in advance: 'You are the master, you are the first among us, you are the happiest of men. You are the victor, as you will always be, Amazonus, you are the victor.' Care was taken to partition off the arena to ease the task of the *emperor-bestiarius*, who at times dispatched a hundred bears in one day. To recover his strength when overcome with weariness in the course of this carnage, he drank chilled honeyed wine which a woman presented to him in a goblet shaped like a mace. Then once more, led by the front rows and then taken up by the whole amphitheatre, resounding vivats rose to the skies. Of course the people were here not applauding a common champion but a god, for as is known Commodus took himself for Hercules. Statues portrayed him with the attributes of the god; he had a lion-skin and a mace paraded before him in the streets and even in his absence they were displayed in the amphitheatre on a gilded dais. Let us add, to complete the portrait, that he never appeared in public without a sword and unless 'covered with human blood'.

But most remarkable was the eagerness which led the emperors to identify themselves very closely with the stars of the arena or the circus by complying with every detail of the customs of the profession. When Nero drove a chariot, he wore the helmet and the dress of the charioteers, even in the presence of foreign kings; on the stage he conformed to all the traditions, except that, when the action required that he should appear chained, golden chains were used. When he returned from Greece having received 1808 crowns, a part of the wall of the city was torn down and the gates taken off at his approach, this being the traditional homage paid to victors crowned at the games. Commodus, who drove only in private, did not even in these circumstances fail to don the livery of the 'Green' faction. Similarly, in the amphitheatre he sometimes gave the people the right of choosing his adversary in accordance with custom. He insisted on being paid every time he fought, the only difference between him and the ordinary gladiators being that he demanded the most fabulous sums. He gloried especially in the fact of being left-handed and caused the following inscription to be engraved on the plinth of the statue of himself: 'The *primus palus secutorum* who, being left-handed, vanquished twelve thousand men on his own, I believe.' Prudence alone limited this desire for 'realism'; his adversaries fought with wooden swords.

The emperors were even imbued with the very psychology of the champion, as the inscription of Commodus proves. Professional jealousies were especially rife among the pantomimists and charioteers; the latter even sometimes appealed to magicians to cast a spell on their adversaries, going so far as quite simply to use poison. Among the emperors these jealousies became morbid and tyrannical. Commodus had Julius Alexander put to death because he had, while on horseback, killed a lion with a javelin. Nero was devoured with uneasiness at the idea that anyone should doubt his talent and by the fear of being defeated by his rivals, whom he actually feared. But he sometimes allowed himself to be vanquished in the circus lest victories should be thought merely formal. This search for authenticity went together with a lunatic sensitivity; it was forbidden to leave the premises when he was singing on the stage. His jealousy did not spare even the glories of the past; one day he challenged Pammenes, famous at the time of Caligula and now stricken in years, simply in order to plume himself on a victory over him and use this as an excuse to have his statues defaced.

A double put to death

Thus while charioteers governed, emperors were bent on playing the part of charioteer. These disconcerting and ostentatious exhibitions were assuredly more than mere buffoonery. Certain religious beliefs may have played their part in them. It is, for the moment, enough for us to show that the desire for realism which the emperors displayed by identifying themselves with champions cannot be explained unless the essential source of this identification is seen to lie in the very popularity of gladiators, *bestiarii* and charioteers. It is clear that the demagogy which sustained the regime favoured this tendency to identification with the idols of the crowd. Besides, have we not seen emperors jealous of the plaudits addressed to a gladiator? Caligula one day expressed the chagrin which he felt in similar circumstances, not in his role of Thracian gladiator upon which he prided himself, but in that of emperor; as the people went on applauding an *essedarius* who had just freed a slave after his victory, he rushed out of the amphitheatre with such fury that he caught his foot in the folds of his toga and fell in the midst of the tiers, shouting with indignation at the people 'who for the most trifling motives gave more honour to a gladiator than to deified emperors or to himself who was present'. It is, moreover, well known that Nero owed his popularity to the immoderate passion which he manifested for the games.

Naturally aristocrats imbued with republican sentiments could not understand that well-bred people should really be fascinated by actors and gladiators, since that sort of admiration reduced them to the level of the populace. For to the Roman of ancient times making an exhibition of oneself in the games for the entertainment of the people was simply a form of prostitution, whatever the nature of the spectacle. In this regard the gladiator represented the nadir of degradation; we have seen, in the story of Eppia and Sergiolus, how this scorn, justified by the law, was backed up by moral prejudices. But there was in this respect no radical difference between this profession and the others; the actor himself was brought to the bar of society. There was nothing more narrow-minded in this regard than the Roman mentality.

The life of French actors under the *ancien régime* was a paradise compared with that of the classical Thespians; by treading the boards they incurred both dishonour and civil degradation. They were, up to a late period, liable to be beaten at all times and in all places. To sum up, a soldier who became an actor was liable to the death penalty. We can understand that, for men imbued with this mentality, the appearance of members of the aristocracy or the emperor himself in a public spectacle was scandalous; hence the eagerness of Suetonius to stress the social standing of gladiators when they had been knights or senators, and the indignation of Tacitus at Nero's prowess.

In so far as traces of this old attitude of mind remained in existence, the relation between the gladiator or the charioteer and his public was not without a certain ambiguity; they were at the same time pariahs and stars. But the examples we have just quoted are enough to prove that these ancient prejudices were no longer very strong under the Empire. Contempt for these men was no longer deeply rooted in social consciousness, as it had been previously; it was expressed only among the 'intellectuals' or the dyed-in-the-wool traditionalists like Juvenal or Tacitus, whose imprecations and arrogant pride certainly did not reflect the opinion of the man-in-the-street. In reality, attitudes had changed; not because the emperors had set themselves up as gladiators or charioteers, something which was a consequence and not a cause of the change, for all that this sort of encouragement had undeniably hastened the process; but because the public, which had renounced the right to impose its opinions, had ended by imposing its tastes, aided therein by all those who had an interest in flattering it and in being in the swim.

As evidence of this change we note that writers of fiction are only too eager to make much of the fascination exercised by the gladiator or the charioteer, going so far as to turn the one or the other into the ideal hero of conventional love-stories. Juvenal has already given us a realistic version of the passion inspired by a gladiator, thus bearing witness to the prestige of these swashbucklers. Here is another version, deeply imbued, despite its cruelty, with poetic idealism:

'Faustina, daughter of Antoninus Pius and wife of Marcus Aurelius, having seen the gladiators pass one day, conceived the most violent love for one of them; and this passion having made her ill for a long time, she confessed it to her husband. Chaldeans whom Marcus Aurelius consulted said that it was necessary that this gladiator should be killed and that Faustina should bathe in his blood and afterwards lie with her husband. When this advice had been followed, the empress' passion was in fact spent, but she brought into the world Commodus, who was more of a gladiator than a prince. . . .'

Let us pass over the strangeness of this ancient version of the werewolf, which was presumed to account for the monstrous behaviour of Commodus, and over the comments to which the remedies counselled to Marcus Aurelius might inspire psychologists. Everything in this tale combines to make it a tragedy of which the gladiator, capable of arousing a superhuman and also, to be sure, an unhappy passion, is the hero: the chance encounter (Faustina sees the *pompa* as it passes and it is the face of one man amongst so many others marching past her which overcomes her), the uncontrollable violence of her feelings and its suddeness; the exhaustion of a long illness, the confession, the recourse to the oracles and in the end the sacrifice carried out with barbaric sensuality, in comparison with which the libations of Phaedra seem innocent. All this to explain the simple fact that Faustina, like so many other women in Rome, had fallen in love with a gladiator.

In a somewhat similar vein, Dio Cassius is at pains to note 'the very strange circumstances' in which Elagabalus fell in love with the charioteer Hierocles. It is, all things considered, another version of love at first sight, somewhat similar to the preceding one: 'Hierocles, during the games in the circus, fell from his chariot directly in front of the seat of Elagabalus. As he fell, his helmet came off. Noticed by the prince—he had a beardless chin and long, fair hair—he was immediately picked up and taken to the palace.' Here the sudden revelation takes place most poetically in a flash at the very moment of the fall.

Thus the famous gladiators and charioteers no longer aroused only the somewhat scornful admiration given to virtuosi taking part in the entertainments conceived for the public taste. They were flattered as heroes capable of inspiring people with super-human emotions. The fascination which they exercised was dreaded. Though they sometimes fell victim to the vanity which overcame the emperor, either *in propria persona* or in his capacity of rival, they could also do so to the jealousy with which they filled him as a man. The horrible end of the gladiator loved by Faustina was not an isolated case. Claudius had Mnester, lover of Messalina, put to death and Domitian had the pantomimist Paris, of whom his wife was enamoured, killed. Just as Nero had wished to tear down the statues of Pammenes so this emperor laid hands on the very image Paris had left behind him. He had one of his pupils put to death, though he had not reached puberty and was ill at the time, because 'his performance and his person too closely recalled those of his master', going so far, as we see, as to protect himself against his unlikely survival. At other times it was the partisan who disposed of a man whose fame was resented as an insult to the opposing faction; Caligula, who fanatically supported the Thracians, one day had poison poured into the wounds of a gladiator called Columbus simply because he was a *myrmillo*.

At the time at which the games reached the high point of their development, the champions of the arena therefore broke from their condition of chattels or merchandise, and by enter-taining the public became fetishes upon which a semi-idle society concentrated its passions, its erotic or warlike fantasies. Hero

21(a) Mask of a gladiator in sheet bronze from the amphitheatre at Rodez, now at the Fenaille Museum at Rodez. (Photo Louis Balsan)

21(b) Combat between women: Amazona and Achillia do not wear helmets, doubtless because the public wanted to see the faces of these unusual stars. British Museum. (Photo R. B. Fleming)

22(a) Gladiators portrayed on a Roman lamp found in England. It was thus that the career of many came to an end. Lamp, British Museum. (Photo R. B. Fleming)

22(b) A civilization based on the games: at Pula in Dalmatia, the taste for blood went side by side with the refinements of a seaside resort. (Photo Boudot-Lamotte)

worship went as far as veneration; did not a man one day hurl himself onto the funeral pyre of a charioteer?

A miserable fate

Such is the flattering image of the gladiator or the charioteer which literature has handed down to us, and such, doubtless, in some measure was the idea which the Romans themselves had of them. But it goes almost without saying that this picture cannot tally with the facts. To 'produce' a few stars, the market of the games had first to absorb a considerable number of men whose fate had nothing in common with that of the privileged ones we have just described.

If one keeps strictly to what actually was the case, what strikes one is precisely the fact of the enormous disparity between the condition of the tiro and that of the veteran. This, first of all, was due to the smallness of the enrolment bonus, the derisory nature of which we have already noted. It represented about a seventh part of what a veteran received on re-enrolment. Doubtless the fixing of so low a tariff was intentional in order to prevent, or at least restrain, the enrolment of honourable citizens deprived of resources, whom the lure of more substantial gains might have drawn in droves to the gladiatorial schools. One wonders, however, to what degree this was decisive, since, in fact, a discrimination based on the social origin of the gladiator, or on any other criterion, for that matter, could assuredly have provided similar guarantees without resulting in the implication which to the Romans was a natural consequence of such a system (though it may shock the modern mind)—that human life is cheap. The gladiator was paid—when indeed he was paid—in his capacity of professional performer—not as a man who regularly risked his life. Thus the *lanista* always had a source of cheap raw material to hand.

The rewards in money that the novice or the beginner could hope for from his victories in the arena—or, if you like, his combat bonus—were far from sufficient to compensate him for this initial absence of earning power, for they were proportional to the price paid by the *editor* for the gladiator himself and thus unquestionably depended on the value of his skill. Whether this reward was a fifth or a quarter of this price, depending on whether a slave or a free man was in question, it could not exceed a few hundred sesterces for mediocre gladiators, which beginners, with very rare exceptions, almost certainly were. It is obvious that two years' training did not give a man mastery over champions tempered by thirty or so victories and experienced in all the tricks of swordsmanship. The amassing of a few rewards was far from assuring a future to a gladiator with several years of his professional life already behind him.

An official tariff introduced by Marcus Aurelius to prevent speculation will give us a pretty clear idea of the disparities which could exist in this field, and of which account was taken on a quite different level by matching none but gladiators of similar strength and experience. It drew a distinction between the *promiscua multitudo* (or *gregarii*), that is to say the mass of poorly qualified men, many of whom would be called upon to lay down their lives without glory in their first encounters, and the *meliores* or *summi gladiatores* who had already been put to the test. Now we note that within this last class alone, which itself included several categories, the price of a gladiator, and consequently his combat bonus, given him on a percentage basis, varied from 500 to 3,000 sesterces. It is not difficult to imagine what fell to the share of the worst of the *gregarii*.

For several years, therefore, aside from these bonuses which, all in all, amounted to a truly pitiable wage, the gladiator could expect to make no more than bed and, if one may so put it, board. The *lanista*, in effect, assured him his day-to-day existence. This fact explains the prevalence of the prejudice that a gladiator was a mere slave of his belly; and if things were considered simply in terms of their effects, unrelated to whatever else had helped to bring the wretched fellow to this pass, that in truth was what it amounted to—bread in exchange for slavery and death.

It may fairly be asked if such a life was worth living. The most romantic ideas and the most realistic concerns meet here. We should like to know, in particular, if barrack life in the *ludus* allowed of any sort of normal existence and what in this institution made it better than life in a convict prison or a fire station. Our sources scarcely allow us to descend to this level. No 'evidence' similar to that with which literature teems has been handed down to us, save for a few graffiti. The *ludus* of Pompeii has yielded nothing but skeletons and the mystery of a woman covered with gold and precious stones, stretched out in the midst of eighteen gladiators. The only account that we have of life in the *ludus* occurs in the course of a declamation which stresses only the most conventional themes: 'I was no longer thin and disfigured,' says a young man of good family captured at sea and sold to a *lanista*, 'as I was when in the hands of the pirates; the good cheer that I found there was more intolerable to me than hunger; I was being fattened up like a sacrificial victim; and, scum among condemned slaves, I was a raw gladiator learning every day how to commit murder.' All in all, only the inscriptions allow us to glean a few positive items of information.

Many of the gladiators were married, others supported a family. It has been conjectured, doubtless correctly, that in such cases they did not live in the *ludus* but in the town and that only the unmarried ones were in barracks. Some enrolled at seventeen or eighteen and died quite young, having just passed their twentieth year, like Juvenis at Padua. Only rarely did a gladiator who had reached the age of thirty have fewer than a score of combats to his credit. At that age, one of them had fought thirty-four times. This is not to say that he had as many victories. Thus the honours list of Flamma reads as follows: out of a total of thirty-four combats he had won twenty-one, had been *stans missus* nine times, that is to say sent back after an indecisive combat, and on four occasions *missus*, that is to say vanquished, owing his life only to the generosity of the spectators.

It is difficult to be sure how often the gladiator had to face death. As the *munera* lasted several days, and sometimes as long as a month, a gladiator often had to fight twice in the course of a single *munus*. Thus Felix, twice opposed to the same *retiarius*, at a few days' interval, and twice beaten, was first reprieved by the crowd and then condemned. But it does not seem that gladiators were made to go down a great number of times into the arena in the course of any one year or fixed period of time. Juvenis, for example, who died at twenty-one after four years in the *ludus*, fought only five combats and those who died between the ages of twenty and twenty-five fought only seven times. This average is probably not due to the fact that these men were beginners, for it agrees roughly with that for men who had reached their thirties. It seems in any case reasonable to grant that gladiators did not have to enter the arena more than two or three times a year.

Solidarity in misfortune

'Bad luck' could show itself first of all in the shape of the opponent chosen by lot. For even if the gladiators who were paired were of roughly equal strength, there were some who had acquired a reputation for invincibility that caused their very name to be dreaded. A graffito on the barracks at Pompeii tells us, for example, that two gladiators had been picked to fight against the *essedarius* Amaranth, and the author of the inscription adds: 'Let them tremble.' It was bad luck also to die of wounds after having overcome one's opponent; this happened often enough, as is proved by the inscriptions, according to which the man who had thus died had—what a consolation!—the privilege of calling himself *invictus*, unconquered. Then there were the moments of weakness arising from age, when the body begins to lose its elasticity and the arm becomes less sure, from not being 'on form'. In such cases, the *cena libera* became transformed into a sort of ambush. This was the last meal given to the gladiators on the eve of the fight, at which they could eat and drink their fill and which could fatally stupefy them for the morrow's trial. 'Weakness', moreover, was often a euphemism for defeat; the vanquished had been 'surprised', 'deceived by fate', 'betrayed'.

Death delivered very many from the cares of the future. In the gladiators' cemetery are numberless epitaphs sounding the baleful roll of all the nations of the world: '*Generoso, Retiario invicto . . . natione Alexandrinus*', '*Amabili secutori, natione Dacus. . . .*' Men from Modena lay there beside those who came from Phrygia. Where a widow did not care for the mortal remains, the *familia gladiatoria*, or even a comrade of the dead man, did so; it was a sacred duty, for which the gladiators clubbed together or even formed associations. The headstone almost always bears an epitaph, an honours list sometimes accompanied by a short biography or an indication of the circumstances of the man's death. Sometimes it is decorated with a portrait of the gladiator, standing armed, his helmet resting on a column or on his arm. A dog found on several monuments sitting guilelessly at the feet of the solemn warrior, intrigues and moves one, as one wonders whether it is to be understood as a symbol of faithful companionship.

But what did the future offer those who survived after their contract had run its term? We do not know after how many years or how many combats the gladiator was free of all obligation. He had to receive the *rudis*, the wooden sword which the people sometimes demanded for those who managed to win its favours. If he were a slave, he did not for all this gain his liberty, for he still had to obtain his emancipation. As for the criminal, his reward was no longer to have to appear in the arena, though he had to complete his sentence in the *ludus*, by doing some job or other. In fact only the free man who had enrolled was finally liberated on receipt of the *rudis*; when this happened he went ceremonially to lay down his arms in the temple of Mars. But afterwards?

The minority of successful gladiators and of those with a long experience of the profession had the choice of retirement or a sinecure. There were former gladiators who ended their lives as peaceful smallholders in the country. If they had not managed to save enough to live thus on their income, they could always become instructors (*doctores*) at the barracks, which was always ready to pay for their experience, and where some of them lived to a ripe age. Finally, if the temptation of taking up their profession once again overcame them, they could at least charge very heavily for their services.

But by far the greater number of second-rate gladiators, short of struggling to make a problematic return to civil life on very slender means, were faced with either re-enlisting or penury. Alongside the *nouveaux riches* veterans one found others who were beggars. A still young and healthy man was positively driven to re-enlist. The temptation was the same as at roulette; on the one hand, by leaving the profession he recovered the right to dispose of the life which he had staked, but on the other hand he had staked his all for nothing, since he found himself, roughly speaking, in the same situation as before. But to the optimism to which his semi-success could prompt him there was added a decisive incentive—on re-enlisting he would this time get a large bonus.

For men willing to endure so harsh a present with no guarantee of a better future there were, as we have seen, possible strokes of luck. But there was also the 'spirit' of the barracks or, so to speak, a sort of fellowship with which the novice very quickly became imbued and which could help him to accept certain things. Its essential feature was a rather special code of honour; the gladiator, for example, refused to fight against an adversary whom he did not consider his equal. His motto was in fact summed up in a phrase recorded in an epitaph: 'Many fights, many victories.' Seneca reports having heard the *myrmillo* Triumphus at the time of Tiberius complain about not going into the arena often enough because the emperor did not give more *munera* than the number strictly prescribed by law. 'What a waste of good time', he said. It is superfluous to repeat once more what we have already said about the steadfastness which all knew how to show in the face of death.

Esprit de corps and a certain sense of comradeship were defences against the harshness of their conditions. The advice engraved on the tomb of a gladiator who had had his throat cut by an opponent whom he had spared in a former encounter: 'No pity for the vanquished' does not seem to reflect the usual mentality of the *ludus*. The petty rivalries and ferocious jealousies so frequent among the charioteers were not the rule in the *ludus*; quite the contrary, the last honours were scrupulously paid to a departed comrade and, if the opportunity presented itself, he was avenged in fair fight. The feeling of honour and *esprit de corps* formed part of the glorification of manly virtue.

VII

A CIVILIZATION BASED ON THE GAMES

'*Panem et circenses*'

The idea of spectacles as we know them was alien to the Romans.
A spectacle did not, in fact, represent for them an entertainment
intended for the pleasure of a casual audience. It was impossible
to conceive at Rome any enterprise so commonplace as the opening of a theatre. The organization of spectacles was a sort of
public service. The role of private initiative was limited to providing the officials responsible with the means of staging a programme the main lines of which had been laid down in advance.
This seems astonishing in a society in which state control was yet
not the rule. The reason is that the spectacles at first had no
legitimate function *per se*; they had something sacred about them,
and everything that in any way concerned religion was at Rome
subject to strict state control.

It was therefore normal that the spectacles should have been
called upon to play the essential role in political life we have
acknowledged them to have. The Empire turned them into a
well-known instrument of domination, clearly defined by
Juvenal in his phrase *panem et circenses*, which has remained
famous. Bread, naturally, implied spectacles; once idleness was
given the stamp of official approval, it became necessary to amuse
the plebs, lest they should fall a prey to moods dangerous to the
totalitarian power which had just been set up. It had long been
known that the more the public shouted itself hoarse at the circus,
the less importance its voice had in the assemblies. The custom
of the games, which the Republic, wearied of itself, had be-

184

queathed to the new regime, was in the nature of an obligation which it could not avoid. They were just what was needed, a first-rate means of keeping people amused, and the rulers used it deliberately and skilfully; it was for them a well-proven technique.

We cannot study here in detail the reasons for this state of affairs; we must limit ourselves to presenting a sort of X-ray.

The sacrifice to leisure

No emperor allowed himself to neglect the spectacles completely. There was one celebrated recalcitrant, Tiberius, who, as Jérôme Carcopino remarks, was really the last of the Republicans. He refrained from giving the people those extraordinary spectacles which, like the *munera,* were an expression of sheer liberality, evidence of goodwill and solicitude. Openly remaining aloof from the people, he even reduced the budget of the annual games and curtailed the number of pairs of gladiators allowed to appear in a single show. But, and this must be stressed, these pin-pricks, more symbolic than real, did not prevent the Romans from benefiting from all the games sanctioned by tradition and which the emperor did not have the audacity to suppress. There were others who were lukewarm, like Marcus Aurelius, who found the vulgarity of crowding elbow to elbow on the tiers amid blood and dust disgusting. That, however, did not prevent him from making arrangements to ensure that the populace should not be deprived of its *munera* whenever he left Rome. Otherwise, from Augustus to Trajan, the emperors merely outbid one another in the splendour and number of feast-days.

It was not enough to give games; it was also necessary to attend them and to show to advantage at them. As much as on the quality and number of the games he gave and on the trouble he took to assure their success, the popularity of an emperor depended on the human factor, on the way he behaved in the midst of the crowd. It was not enough for him to preside at these entertainments; what the crowd liked above all was the fact that he shared its passions and showed that he found his pleasure where it found its own.

It has long been noted that the popularity which Nero enjoyed after his death, which lasted sufficiently long to give rise to impostors who made use of his name, can only be explained by his taste for the spectacles and his eagerness to provide them. To win the favour of his subjects the emperor, once he had taken his seat, had to banish all semblance of reserve and even, as we should say today, do his best to become 'one with the people'. So much so that we see the best of the princes taking the basest creatures as their example; in the gladiatorial combats Titus noisily supported the Thracians and apostrophised their adversaries with gibes worthy of a bargee. Claudius proved himself, through simplicity it is true and not by calculation, a model in this respect:

'There was no spectacle' [the *munera* are referred to] 'in which he appeared more affable and more gay; he could be seen, in the manner of the vulgar, counting on his fingers at the top of his voice the gold pieces offered to the victor. He would urge all the spectators to enjoy themselves, calling them his 'masters' from time to time, and larding his remarks with jokes in fairly bad taste. . . . But what was liked above all was that he wrote notices addressed to the crowd on tablets and had these circulated among the spectators, instead of having them transmitted by means of heralds as was customary.'

The attitude of Augustus, whose conservatism was well known, is perhaps the most characteristic in this connection. In his will he did not fail to enumerate, alongside the reforms which he had effected, the games with which he had gratified the people, either in his own name or in the names of those close to him. We know from Suetonius that he made a point of attending the games, and of doing nothing there apart from watching the spectacle, since he had noticed that the people had taken it ill that Caesar used to dispatch his business in the arena and even profit from this moment of relaxation to write letters.

Why was it that even the sanest of the emperors carried this concern with the games to the point of sycophancy? Fronto, in the sententious language that characterises him, was more successful in bringing the mainspring of the policy into full relief than was Juvenal with his succinct phraseology. After praising Trajan for the attention which he always took care to show to the professionals of the stage, the circus or the arena, he adds that

'. . . the excellence of a government is shown no less by its concern for pastimes than by its concern for serious matters, negligence being, it is true, far more prejudicial in the latter, but creating far more dissatisfaction in the former: *that the people are, all in all, less avid for money than for spectacles*; and that though distributions of corn and foodstuffs are enough to satisfy men as individuals, spectacles are needed to satisfy the people as a whole.'

Let us note first that this analysis quite clearly shows the communal and specific character of this need. We have seen that at the amphitheatre or at the circus, the pleasure experienced by the crowd was not limited simply to the games; it arose also from the collective self-consciousness which came into being, from an obscure narcissism to which the consciousness of oneself as a Roman was not irrelevant.

Its essential merit however was to affirm the paradoxical priority of games over bread. This is a phenomenon that is easily explainable; the spectacle was all the more the sacred to the plebs in that it represented a luxury, the only one they had. A grain shortage or an interruption in the distribution of food-stuffs could provoke violent and immediate reactions among the people, who were usually pacified by the sacrifice of some scapegoat. Once the situation returned to normal, there remained hardly a trace of this ephemeral and noisy discontent. Not so, however, when the spectacles were neglected, no matter whether the neglect was deliberate or not. This provoked sullen, stubborn, and smouldering rancour, more dangerous than a riot; for the disaffection of the people created a climate favourable to the attempts of usurpers. There was in fact no reason why the people should not exchange for another a master who scorned what every poor Roman regarded as his right and, in the strict sense of the word, his privilege—to take his seat almost daily at the amphitheatre or the circus.

With the colossal sums which were spent in these two places he could have been assured of more than a strict minimum living standard. But that would have suited nobody's book; to maintain the balance of society living standards were sacrificed to leisure.

The people and the image of the god-emperor

People have rightly stressed that the games gave the emperor the chance of establishing with the Roman people the contact indispensable to the smooth functioning of a regime that was at once authoritarian and demagogic; that the amphitheatre and the circus had become assemblies where the people spontaneously made its wishes known to the emperor. The spectators would repeatedly shout the name of a gladiator whose appearance or emancipation they desired. They would even take the liberty of demanding a reduction in taxes or the abrogation of a law. Sometimes, instead of welcoming them in a friendly manner as was usually done, they went so far as to show hostility towards the emperor's favourites, or even towards the emperor himself.

However, these 'democratic exchanges' had certain limits, let it be said at once. One day, when Domitian was presiding at a gladiatorial combat, he refused to reprieve a Thracian beaten by a *myrmillo* because he favoured the latter class of fighter. Whether it was the manifest injustice of the decision or whether there was among the spectators a man who was as fanatical a supporter of the Thracians as the emperor was of the *myrmillones*, one of them shouted that 'a Thracian was a match for a *myrmillo* but not for the giver of the games', thus stigmatising the arbitrary nature of the decision and its evident partiality. Domitian, thus taunted, had the man seized immediately. He was torn from his seat, a placard was fixed to his back and 'having been transformed from a spectator into a spectacle', was at once thrown into the arena to the mob. On the placard was written: 'A favourer of the Thracians who spoke impiously.' It was a surprising ground for resentment but one which is made clearer if one recalls that Domitian often began his edicts with the words: 'Our master and our god commands as follows. . . .' He had seen in this criticism addressed to one of his gladiators evidence of more than scorn for his person—an insult to his divinity.

Domitian, it is true, was the most authentic of tyrants. He had a deep hatred of the people. He insisted on being accompanied to all the gladiatorial combats by a 'youth' (*puerulus*) with a stunted and deformed head who went draped in purple and whom he made to sit at his feet. He joked with him continually and sometimes even talked with him quite seriously, asking for example: 'Can you guess why I have just appointed Mettius Rufus prefect of Egypt?' The quite evident objectivity of Suetonius leaves one in no doubt about the significance of this attitude; it was a way of showing contempt for the audience, even of ignoring its very existence.

But what then? The barbarity of which he gave proof that day is not as illogical as it seems. It revealed the hidden nature of the relation which linked the emperor with his people or, if you like, his 'public'. As the organization of the cult of the emperor proves, the spectacles had among other reasons for their existence that of giving substance to the idea of the god-emperor. At the amphitheatre, if the spectator raised his head towards the *velum* sprinkled with stars which protected him from the sun, he saw in the centre, embroidered in purple, the image of Nero driving a chariot; if he lowered his eyes he saw him once again, in his box, and even sometimes on the stage. Furthermore, he was not allowed to take his eyes off him. Whether it rained, or the wind blew, or there was an earthquake, it was a crime to leave the building while Nero was singing.

For, besides being the provider, organizer and president of the games, the emperor sometimes wished to be the star as well. He found in this a perverse means of making his divinity in-

carnate. Of the fact that some of the emperors took their identification with this or that Olympian god seriously there can be no
doubt. But it little mattered after all whether they thought themselves Hercules or Apollo. As has been adequately explained in
the preceding chapter, what they wanted in taking the reins of a
chariot was to become the *living* idol of the crowd: it was the
grotesque interpretation of a political idea, that of a 'divine
privilege', which had proved its efficacy since the time of Caesar.

Once the tyrants were dead, there were protests—witness the
imprecations of the Senate after the assassination of Commodus.
But it is none the less not for this silence that the Roman elite is
especially to be blamed, but for the fact that it allowed massacres
to be perpetrated daily in the arena for the pleasure of the masses.

The 'crime' of the intellectuals

The gladiatorial combats were not the most cruel of all the
spectacles which we have described; the organized butcheries of
the naumachias, the sophisticated tortures of the 'mythological
dramas', in which the deception caused the 'hero' to die in utter
loneliness, not to speak of the mass executions of the condemned
thrown to the beasts, are even more intolerable affronts to our
sensibilities. But the combats are the best known, and therefore
the first to be condemned. However, the possibility of such
censure scarcely ruffled the spirit of the Romans. If they passed
judgement on the gladiatorial combats, it was rather in the
manner in which a modern philosopher might pass judgement
on motor races: casually, and because he happened to find in
them, and in the behaviour of those taking part, material illus-
trative of this or that theory.

There are thus in the works of the Latin authors what could
be considered 'judgements', more or less explicitly stated, but
generally speaking of a similar nature; *they do not condemn,
they even give their approval.* Here, for example, is the opinion
of Cicero:

'I know that in the eyes of some people the gladiatorial

combats are a cruel and inhuman spectacle; and perhaps they are not wrong considering the way in which the combats are given today. But in the days when it was criminals who killed one another, no lesson in how to endure in the face of pain and death could be more efficacious, at least among those addressed not to the ears but to the eyes.'

If we interpret this correctly, it would appear that his only reservation concerns the fact that the gladiators are no longer recruited exclusively among criminals as formerly, and it is in virtue of this and not of the actual principle of the combat that the accusation of cruelty can be justified.

The whole passage, which forms part of a very characteristic line of argument, according to which an upper-class man ought to be able to do what 'a Samnite, a brigand, the lowest of rogues' can do, is a spirited eulogy of the gladiatorial art:

'These gladiators, these rogues, these barbarians, to what lengths do they not carry their strength of mind? Once masters of their profession, do they not prefer to receive a blow to breaking their rules? What evidently concerns them more is the desire to please both their master and the spectators. Covered with wounds, they send to ask their master if he is satisfied; and if he is not they are ready to offer their throats. Has the least proficient ever groaned or shown fear? What art there is in their very downfall itself in order to conceal their shame from the eyes of the public! Thrown down at last at the feet of their opponent, do they turn away their heads if he shows them the sword?'

The courage and, above all, the self-control which they display are, Cicero adds, the fruit of a combination of training, reflection and habit.

Elsewhere, it is true, he shows himself somewhat critical of the cruelties of the *venatio*: 'What pleasure can a cultured man find in seeing some poor devil torn to pieces by a beast of gigantic strength, or a superb animal transfixed by a lance?' But it must not be forgotten, as it often is when this passage is quoted, that it is taken from a letter in which Cicero sets out to denigrate the games at Pompeii, something which considerably reduces the significance of the remark. Let us note, moreover, that the accusation made here is not of cruelty but of frivolity.

Pliny the Younger waxes even more eloquent about the incomparable merits of these spectacles and those taking part: 'We then had occasion to see a spectacle which did not sap the vitality of men or weaken them; one incapable of enfeebling and degrading manly spirits, but of a nature to excite them to bear noble wounds and scorn death and to make the very slaves and criminals give proof of a love of glory and desire for victory'. If Pliny is to be believed, the *munus* would in fact be almost the contrary of a spectacle, since this word, in the traditional outlook of the Romans, is defined precisely as something that saps vitality and weakens; the *munus*, on the contrary, excites to the highest of virtues: courage and the desire for glory. That at least is what normally seems to be understood from these texts.

The judgement of Seneca, which at first glance seems quite contrary to the opinions which we have just quoted, is in reality exceedingly ambiguous. He first of all takes care to distinguish between the gladiatorial combats in the real sense of the term and the summary massacres of which the arena was the scene during the midday interlude. We have seen that these were really disguised executions carried out at a rush. Humanly speaking, these butcheries had nothing in common with the fair combats based on very strict rules, in which the risk of death was the smaller the more the protagonists played the game with conviction, since the valorous loser was usually spared. The indignation shown by Seneca in the letter we have summarized in Chapter II is thus not aimed at the gladiatorial art. We have even less right to call upon his help in the matter in discussion, in that he himself established a clear distinction between these two bloody manifestations. 'To teach [a man] to inflict and receive wounds is impious enough', he says, evidently alluding to the

23(*a*) Fragment of a gladiatorial scene on a Gallo-Roman earthenware vase in the Fenaille Museum at Rodez. (Photo Louis Balsan)

23(*b*) Interior of the amphitheatre at El Djem (Tunisia). (Photo Boudot-Lamotte)

24. Arles. The theatre and the amphitheatre. (Photo Yan)

first-rate training gladiators received from the *lanista*; 'here he is dragged before the public naked and disarmed, and the only exhibition [we demand] of a human being is his death-agony.'

Nothing is thus more false than generalizations based on the midday games. In particular the picture of gladiators driven to combat with whips and branding-irons has something sensational about it and was exceptional; these extreme measures, which were required to send wretched men to the slaughter, assumed in the *munera* a quite exceptional character. The moral code of the profession, the love of arms, the excitement of a real combat, were usually sufficient to ensure the zeal of the protagonists.

This said, the fact remains that Seneca also condemned the gladiatorial combats on several occasions. This Stoic of the court hated the rabble; how then could he have approved of what it admired? According to him, its plaudits were the infallible sign of error, and contact with it was a guarantee of defilement. It had neither human face nor human voice: 'The confused growling of a crowd is to me like the waves, like the sough of the wind which whips the forest, like everything that emits only unintelligible sounds.' He even credits the rabble with faults it did not have; it prefers, he says, the midday fights to the more sophisticated professional combats. That this was not true we know, however, from the degree of technical skill required to satisfy the demands of the crowd and the enthusiasm with which the *postulaticii* were greeted when they made their appearance. Above all, he accuses the spectacle of being, like the crowd which found pleasure in it, inept and frivolous; the moral promiscuity which he implies is the complete opposite of the asceticism without which there can be no wisdom.

It must however be admitted that sometimes, beneath the condemnation of the aristocrat surfeited with contempt for the rabble, one glimpses a feeling of humanity which condemns the taste for human blood and the cruelty of a degenerate people which were exhibited at the *munera*. From this point of view the accusation drawn up by Seneca, based on the idea of respect for the human individual, is very close to the indictment of the

Christians. It is therefore not astonishing that it should have found no echo among the intellectuals with the exception of Tertullian: 'Seneca is often on our side.'

On the other hand, an attitude of ostentatious contempt for the spectacles and especially for the *munera* as manifestations of a stupidity and vulgarity typical of the masses was probably more widespread at Rome than has been generally allowed. It cannot, in any event, be attributed to Seneca alone. Marcus Aurelius, for example, considered the *munera* useless and boring; and conspicuous abstention from the spectacles on the days when the entire city crammed the tiers of the amphitheatre or the circus was a fairly common thing. On such days, the cultured Roman shut himself up at home or took refuge in the countryside and devoted himself to meditation or leisured study; and could scarcely avoid congratulating himself on devoting to such fruitful pastimes the hours which others were losing watching the tedious manoeuvres of two swordsmen or waxing enthusiastic about a rag.

Oddly enough, the men who voice such sentiments are the very ones who, like Pliny or Cicero, elsewhere openly praise the *munera*. In truth, this is perhaps no contradiction. These reservations do not, in fact, appear to be an expression of deep conviction. They have rather the look of philosophical commonplaces. Reading the Stoics closely, one notes their aversion for the imbecile lack of thought and the foolish agitation encouraged by the times. It is besides a literary commonplace, since these reflections always appear among the purple passages in 'the letter', a quite distinct literary form. Such expressions of scorn are not a condemnation of the *munera*; they are little more than an epistolary affectation, comments made in confidence by one aristocrat to another.

All in all, modern historians are perhaps right to consider this tradition of disparagement as of no account and to believe that, with the exception of Seneca, the Roman elite approved of the gladiatorial combats. This attitude seems to them inexplicable; granted that an uneducated and politically brutalized rabble might have acquired a taste for these massacres—but an elite nurtured on Greek philosophy? To try to understand this, they turn to the justifications provided by Pliny or Cicero and what do they find? The gladiatorial combats are a school of valour, they excite the most noble sentiments, the love of glory and the scorn of death. At this point, usually, they either smile or become indignant. It is easy to show the absurdity of such a justification. It is plain to everyone that the passion for these combats was, on the contrary, a sign of political and moral degradation. A people which had lost the habit of being master of its own fate was henceforth content with dressing up in its Sunday best to watch a parody: for as we have seen the arms of gladiators and their fighting techniques, borrowed successively from conquered peoples, were in some sense the fossilized image of the Roman conquests. In this respect the amphitheatre took the place of the historical romance. In the battles between troupes, in the naumachias, in certain historical pageants such as the one given by Claudius in which the capture and sack of a city were re-enacted, the intention was quite clearly to make 'the great moments of history' live again, just as the great moments of legend were made to live again in the 'mythological dramas'.

At these spectacles, to be sure, the people wanted to be entertained, not to be morally uplifted by suitable contact with a world of heroes or fired by example. They were taken, like children, to 'historical performances'. In these they relived their own past in caricature, or found a cheap way of satisfying their lust for cruelty. For watching a struggle to the death between two men while sitting down in safety is surely a strange incitement to bravery; and sending someone to his death by means of a careless gesture, an even stranger one. The sophistry is gross: morally speaking, the habit of playing with impunity with the lives of others could only instil flabbiness; to use a famous phrase—which, from this point of view, so well characterizes the amphitheatre—'Many spectators and few men.'

Unable to explain how men like Pliny or Cicero could have defended so untenable an argument, the historian is apt to turn abruptly into a moralist. For the most part he loses patience, becomes indigant and condemns. It is a way of burying the problem.

From slavery to 'liberty'

For our part, we do not think that the apologies of Pliny and Cicero should be considered mere political devices, or the effect, more or less, of a guilty conscience. Close examination of the texts proves the contrary. Most people see in the passages from the *Tusculan Disputations* previously quoted only an expression of approval or an 'apologia'. Such over-simplification simply distorts the meaning. Cicero states: first that *when criminals were pitted against one another* the *munera* gave an exemplary lesson in strength and courage; but that it is perhaps not wrong to consider them inhuman *in their present form*. What does he mean?

The context leaves no doubt. They may be considered inhuman since in them appear, as gladiators, men who are not criminals, namely, in all probability, free men, for we have not yet reached the stage at which knights and even senators went down into the arena. In short what Cicero admires is the fact that 'rogues' and 'barbarians' give proof of strength of mind, a matter about which he writes at length. Now that is exactly Pliny's opinion. He approves of the *munera* because they cause '*the very slaves and criminals* to give proof of a love of glory and desire for victory'. Finally, it is of a pattern that a similar reasoning should be found in Seneca. Speaking of that German who preferred to die by thrusting his head through the spokes of a wheel which was bearing him to the amphitheatre, he writes: 'You must not think that only great men have been gifted with the strength of mind that breaks the bonds of human servitude. Do not believe that only a Cato can do such a thing, Cato who with his own hand wrenched free the soul he had not been able to put out of reach of the sword. A mighty impulse has enabled men of the meanest estate to come to a place of safety. . . .'

Comparison of these texts make the fundamental idea of their several authors perfectly clear. For them the moral value of the *munera* lay in the fact that they effected a *transmutation* which no Roman would have thought possible. By their means servile bodies, lacking souls, attained to a standard of behaviour which their very nature seemed to rule out. They made the slave the equal not only of the free man but of the hero to whom a particular *type* of outlook was by nature proper. They could literally be said to liberate him from his condition, which was not that of a man but of a chattel or beast. It is quite clearly this paradox, this inversion of categories that struck men of antiquity, insofar as they showed any interest in this question.

Can we expect a Roman, even a cultured Roman, not to reason as a Roman? If we are astonished at the attitude of the Roman elite in this matter, it means only that we are putting the question wrongly. We start from the idea that they should have taken a stand against the cruelties of which we disapprove and, to excuse them, we search desperately for problematic traces of disapproval. We must, on the contrary, start from the idea that such disapproval was out of the question. When we consider the gladiatorial combats according to our own criteria, we are doing no more than applying a cautery to a wooden leg. And the better to condemn them, we remove an institution or a judgement from the context which conditions it in an artificial and thoroughly unhistorical fashion. We consider them out of relation, when the reverse is what is needed to place them in the context of the beliefs and ideas of the Romans. In this way the gladiatorial combats, from being moral monstrosities, become historical monsters. In very truth, the habit of establishing a radical opposition between our judgements and those of the ancients has led us to distort facts by attributing to the judgement of the latter an approximate meaning and a uniformity they do not possess.

As an analysis of the preceding texts shows, the Roman attitude cannot be explained without admitting from the start that it is conditioned by the existence of slavery, that is to say, by the idea that a human being can be simply an instrument. The gladiators were at first criminals. This circumstance, in our eyes, does not excuse the combats. On the contrary it makes them all the more immoral since in our eyes the criminal has, in some undefined manner, come to have a sacred character. We look upon this way of using his life as a disposable object fit for any and every purpose as the crowning outrage. But this idea could not have shocked the Romans; once a slave, the prisoner or the criminal remained an instrument until his death. Even more, free and fair combat gave him the chance of attaining to the status of a man, of acquiring a dignity of which he was, by definition, deprived. It conferred on him what in the eyes of a Roman was the most precious of privileges, the only one really to be envied, that of dying nobly. Which is why the Romans could make these men the equals of Cato, without any figurative intention.

For the Romans the morality of these spectacles lay therefore in what we condemn the most strongly. Nor does it follow that their immorality, insofar as it can be discerned, had the meaning which we attach to it. When Cicero affirms that the *munera* were cruel and inhuman in their present form we instinctively interpret the phrase as an expression of regret that the blood of men who were not criminals should be shed. Can we be so sure? We ourselves see nothing but the blood. But is he not rather thinking of the degradation, of the dishonour, that the condition of being a gladiator meant for a free man, in that he was, legally and morally, reduced to the status of a slave? To the Romans this downfall, the disgrace of which is always stressed by Tacitus and Suetonius in the case of knights and senators, seemed worse than death itself.

In connection with what has been said, it is not simply the idea of slavery and the ideas of the ancients on human individuality that are in question. The individual, even when free, did not belong to himself; he was strictly subordinated to the city. His life, his death, were only episodes in the history of the group. To confront death was not an act of exceptional heroism; it was the normal way of proving oneself a Roman. Men imbued with this mentality could not look upon the constraints suffered by gladiators, or the blood which was shed in the arena with the same eyes as we do. 'We hate', wrote Cicero, 'those weak and supplicating gladiators who, arms outstretched, beg for their lives.'

The change of attitude, for which the progress of philosophy prepared the way from a certain period on, came into conflict, therefore, with these inherited ideas upon which the tradition of the *munera* was firmly founded. It also conflicted with them as expressions of true national sentiment, something they had finally acquired, owing to their popularity and to their growing importance in Roman life. After all that we have said about the role that they played, we cannot see how men who, for all that they belonged to the ruling class, were above all politicians could have resolutely and publicly condemned them. It would have been a strange form of electoral propaganda.

It is therefore not astonishing that the reticence of the ruling class should have gone no further than an aristocratic 'for our part', an opinion that lent itself to fine flights of eloquence but without contact with reality. Cruelty, which amongst us is concealed and sublimated, in Roman society took on the everyday features of an uninhibited gratification; it is a fact that should be explained.

VIII

THE RUINS OF THE CIRCUSES AND AMPHITHEATRES

The circuses

The circuses have failed to withstand the ravages of time. We have seen that even at the Circus Maximus, of which a few tiers still exist in modern Rome, the use of wood, at least as an auxiliary building material, made the structure vulnerable. In the provinces where they had become common this impermanence was the rule for, if one excepts the large cities, the chariot races, because of their high cost, were outstanding events and not daily bread as at Rome. Thus there was no need of monumental buildings erected at great cost, standing empty at some distance from the town. It was there that they were usually built, preferably on the sloping bank of a river—there may possibly have been a circus of this kind in Paris on the site of the former *Halle aux vins*— that is, where advantage was not taken of the undulating ground to reduce construction costs, something which made it even less likely that the structure would last for any length of time. Circuses, all the same, were far less common than theatres or amphitheatres, precisely because of the high cost of the races.

All that remains of them in the Gallic provinces, for instance, is a few ruins. The best known is the pyramid called the 'needle' which decorated the *spina* of the Vienne circus, which at one time stood between the present rue Vimaise and the Avignon road, on the banks of the Rhône. This 'pyramid', however, which rests on a square base decorated with arcades and columns, is not the obelisk which originally adorned the city circus but a sort of ersatz erected at the end of the third century to replace the first one, probably broken to pieces during the invasions. It stands, at present, on the very site of the circus, of which several stones were found in the nineteenth century, as well as the statue of a satyr pouring water into an urn which probably also decorated the *spina*.

The obelisk at Arles, on the other hand, which was found serving as a bench in a garden before being solemnly erected in the Place de la Republique, is certainly the one which adorned the circus of the town, situated in the present suburb of la Roquette. Probably constructed in the first century A.D., this circus was of considerable size: 100 yards wide by 389 yards long (the Great Circus at Rome measured 109 yards by 656 yards). Only the foundations have been discovered, whereas at Nîmes one can still see today, at the corner of the Rue de Mail and the Place Montcalm, a bare wall which once belonged to the circus of the town, even more imposing than that of Arles, since it seems that it was 547 yards long.

Trèves, Lyons and Saintes also had their own circuses, of which nothing remains. In this last town, however, which at least in the early days of the Empire was the capital of Aquitaine, some very special circumstances led to the discovery of the site. In 1944 the Germans forced the people of Saintes to dig anti-tank traps. This resulted in the discovery of three ditches, one of which contained a mixture of fragments of human skulls and horses' teeth. This was, it is believed, the cemetery reserved for victims of accidents in the circus. The discovery of several tiers made it possible to pinpoint the circus itself in the valley of La Combe the sides of which formed a natural seating area.

In fact the only really suggestive vestiges which remain to us of the circuses are the mosaics found in the provinces, of which some represent the local circuses, some that of Rome. We have already mentioned those of Piazza Armerina and of Carthage. Others are to be found at Gafsa and Volubilis (this one in the style of a parody), and at Barcelona, Gerona and Italica in Spain. The most characteristic theme of these works of art, though not the only one, is a sort of 'snapshot' of the races, which depicts their most spectacular episodes. One of the most beautiful, the mosaic at Lyons which was formerly preserved in the museum at Fourvière, probably represents the local circus whose existence is vouched for by an inscription; it shows the fourth lap of a race. Around a *spina* of an original type formed by two basins, eight chariots bearing the colours of the factions dispute the prize with varying degrees of good fortune; two of them have 'shipwrecked'.

History and legend of the ruins

Few ruins have so well attested a history as those of the numerous amphitheatres whose stones have survived the downfall of the Roman Empire. The history of the Colosseum is, from this standpoint, a model. It was first of all used as a fortress by the Frangipani, soldiers of note closely involved in the internecine quarrels of the thirteenth century, and continually as a quarry by the Roman grandees in need of palaces, in particular Paul III, who used its travertine blocks to build the Farnese Palace. Owing to their vast size, they were fated to be 'used' for these two purposes; and this became more or less the rule. Thus at Fréjus the Saracens seized the amphitheatre in order to turn it into a fortress. After their departure care was taken to destroy it in order to prevent other war-leaders from using it for the same purpose; finally, as was also done at Bourges, the last of its stones were used in the building of the fortifications.

The peculiarity of the Colosseum is that it lent itself to other more or less unexpected purposes. A great *corrida* was given in it; mystery plays were performed there, as they were at Bourges, where in 1536 a mystery 66,000 lines in length was staged with a cast of 500 persons. It was used as a hospital and narrowly escaped being transformed into a factory. For all that, the edifice —more and more dilapidated—where the Christians had gone to their death remained a place of pilgrimage. With Chateaubriand and Byron meditation among these ruins even became one of the essential stages in a journey to the East. Even before this time, moneys collected from the great numbers of pilgrims were used for the construction of a chapel built on the *podium*, which was entrusted to the care of a holy hermit who was even authorized to let the grass which grew in the arena.

It is probable, moreover, that the Colosseum was more than once divided into housing lots. In some pictures washing can be seen drying on the walls, and the inhabitants have opened their window-cum-door formed by a panel of wood fixed across one of the arcades. During the Middle Ages the spot did not have a good reputation. In the words of Friedländer:

'In many places it [the amphitheatre] was handed over to prostitution which made it the scene of most vulgar orgies. These half-collapsed arches and galleries choked with debris provided the outcasts of society with the lairs they sought and many a crime was committed in its mysterious recesses. People combed through the debris in the hope of finding buried treasure or coming across what remained of the ancient splendour of these monuments amidst dismal and ill-famed ruins where sorcerers as well as exorcists naturally found occasion to carry on their mysterious practices. It is enough in this connection to recall Benvenuto Cellini's description of the witchcraft he witnessed in the Colosseum.'

This description self-evidently belongs to the nineteenth century. But we must admit that the amphitheatres, particularly once all that remained of them was debris of unknown origin, seem to have become the centre of superstitions and popular legends. At Bordeaux the amphitheatre, known as the 'Palais Gallien', served as a duelling ground and was believed to be the place where the Devil held his assizes; at Toulon the site on which the amphitheatre rose, now fallen into oblivion, was called the 'claux del diable' or 'the dragon's vineyard'.

The provincial amphitheatres

We will not refer here to the Colosseum or the principal amphitheatres of Italy which have been described at length in Chapter

11. We should need a whole book to describe, even summarily, all the ruins which exist in the provinces, so widespread were the amphitheatres. In north Africa, for example, where we have already become acquainted with a certain number, from that of Carthage, reduced virtually to rubble, to that of El Djem which is undoubtedly the most interesting for the visitor, one has been recently discovered at Lixus in Morocco, a country which had previously been thought not to have had any.

The extent of their diffusion is especially noticeable in the Gallic provinces where the gladiatorial combats were in some places perhaps grafted on to ancient local customs. There are, first of all, those amphitheatres of which we can no longer see anything because they have been absorbed into the buildings of modern towns; thus at Metz the great amphitheatre is buried under the railway station, whereas at Limoges the ruins came to light as a succession of fragments which were immediately destroyed or integrated into the town. Others exist in the form of shapeless ruins, as at Besançon, where a few scraps of wall stand by themselves in the countryside, at Béziers, where the amphitheatre, still an imposing sight in the seventeenth century, is today no more than a mass of hovels on the flanks of the hill of St Jacques overhanging the sheds which have invaded the 'arena'; at Bordeaux, which had an amphitheatre of considerable proportions, only a gateway and a few arcades have been preserved.

Amongst those which have completely disappeared are some of the largest in Gaul, that of Poitiers, capital of Aquitaine, after Saintes, whose major axis was 170 yards, and that of Autun, of roughly similar proportions. Of the first, the arena of which is now occupied by the market of Saint-Hilaire, a few traces remain; of the second we know only the site and parts of the history, to which we shall return later.

Of much greater interest to the visitor is the amphitheatre of Saintes, a few arcades and a gateway of which still rise outside the town. Built in the time of Claudius, it could seat about 20,000 spectators. It rested against the side of a valley, the slopes of which provided a natural foundation for the tiers. This method of construction, which permitted great economies, was extremely widespread. It is to be seen, for example, with certain variations, in the amphitheatre at Trèves. Here, in fact, since the lie of the land did not provide the same natural advantages, a hillock was formed by using the material excavated in the digging of the arena, and in the course of the works on the slope of the Petersberg hill against which one side of the amphitheatre rested. This technique of 'rational' construction reduced the architectural elements properly speaking to an enclosure wall, the entrance passages and the *podium*. Only a few fragments remain of this amphitheatre which once served as a bastion; the arena has been transformed into a square. On the periphery have been found rooms of a sort in which the beasts were kept, and passages in which the machinery was housed.

These remains, however, are unimpressive compared with the amphitheatres at Nîmes and Arles, which time has to a great extent spared. In these two towns, as Grenier stresses, 'The monument makes its impression by the harmony of its proportions and the perfect balance between the shade of its arcades and the brilliance of their setting.' These arenas, in fact, owe nothing to the contours of the terrain. As at Pozzuoli or the Colosseum, they rise from level ground on their own foundations.

The older of these amphitheatres—which may date from the time of Augustus—is that of Nîmes. It is also the better preserved, for the attic storey has not disappeared. Situated in the heart of the ancient town, it measures 150 yards along its major axis and 111 yards along its minor. Even though it is 'in the grand style' it is still a less imposing monument than the Colosseum or the amphitheatre at Pozzuoli, or than those of Poitiers and Autun which have now disappeared. It was entered by a vaulted semicircular gallery whose arcades led alternately to the lower tiers and, by way of a staircase, to the upper ones. Inside, the arrangement was roughly similar to that of the Colosseum: *podium* and *moeniana*, separated by *baltei*. Vomitories gave access to the tiers and staircases led from the galleries, becoming larger as they went down in order to prevent too great a crush. At the very top of the structure, but on the outside, one can still see the brackets pierced by holes which held the masts of the *velum*. Let us say at once that this amphitheatre was not intended for naumachias; such drains as have been discovered were quite simply drainage channels.

Perhaps we owe the exceptional state of preservation of this monument to the special circumstances of its history. It was never left unoccupied. At first, the Visigoths made it into a stronghold which they encircled with a moat and reinforced with two towers which were demolished at the beginning of the nineteenth century. The Saracens then made use of it against Charles Martel who succeeded in expelling them by force of arms after having vainly tried to do so by fire. It then became the refuge of a military order, and finally of the people of Nîmes. The inhabitants of this 'quarter' who at that time numbered about 2,000 souls were, it seems, distinguishable by a particular accent. It is said that Francis I, in 1533, was so moved to admiration by the grandiose appearance of these 'antiquities' that he crawled on the stones on his hands and knees to decipher the inscriptions and gave orders that the houses which littered the edifice be destroyed. But nothing was done about it.

The amphitheatre of Arles, roughly the same size as that of Nîmes (major axis 149 yards, minor 117 yards) was built about half a century later and is so similar in construction that it might have been designed by the same architect. Built on a rocky spur right inside the ancient town, it could seat about 25,000 people. The attic storey has disappeared. On the other hand, three of the square towers, with which it was flanked in the twelfth century in order to transform it into a fortress, still exist. The arena, deeply excavated, could house machinery over which a floor served the gladiators as a duelling ground. The front facing of the tiers has ferns engraved on it at two-yard intervals to mark off the seats. There can even be seen, on the first *balteus*, seats permanently reserved for the oil-merchants of the city by order of the decurions.

A few words should also be said about the amphitheatres of

Toulouse and Lyons. To tell the truth, it is doubtful if the former, of which a few fragments overgrown with bushes have survived at Lardenne, a little over two miles from Toulouse, was really the amphitheatre of that city. It had in effect only 5,000 seats. Furthermore, it was very badly built; excavated material was used to put it up and the *cavea* was supported not by arches but by wooden scaffolding. How can one account for the use of such poor materials in an important city? We do not know. Investigations have revealed that the area round about was fairly densely populated, so that it was perhaps only a supplementary or a suburban amphitheatre.

The second, that of Lyons, has long been sought because the celebrated executions which took place there have confirmed its existence. It is, moreover, alleged to have been found in a great many places in which it manifestly was not. No trace of it was found in the course of thorough searches carried out on the hill of Fourvière which unearthed the theatre and the odeum. It was a stroke of luck that brought it to light. Following up a drainage project, workmen discovered some large flagstones on which a dedicatory inscription was engraved; it gave the name of the builder (Caius Julius Rufus, priest of Augustus) and its approximate date: it was erected under Tiberius in A.D. 19. It was thus clear that this amphitheatre, the remains of which are now being excavated by Audin and Guey, was the oldest in Gaul.

An economical formula; the theatre-amphitheatre

One can count up to roughly thirty amphitheatres properly so called in the Gallic provinces. There were assuredly more. But for the small towns which already had to provide funds for a theatre a second building meant a heavy burden. There were several solutions to this problem. The construction of the edifice could be limited to the tiers which it was possible to set up against the slope of a hill; this provided a more or less 'complete' amphitheatre according to whether the *cavea* (the total area of the tiers) made up a semi-circle or not. It was also possible to build a composite structure, a single 'theatre' which could be used for several purposes. Technically, the theatre-amphitheatres to which this need for economy had given birth were of various types and their classification poses complex problems, including those of terminology, which do not concern us. Some are more like amphitheatres, some more like theatres. We shall limit ourselves to the most characteristic of them.

The originality of the amphitheatre of Senlis lies in the fact that it is a real amphitheatre to which a stage has been added. It is outside the town in a depression known as the Trou de la Fosse. It is small (the major axis of the arena is 46 yards). The stage, 12 yards long, occupied a paved space embedded in the *podium*. A more or less similar formula was used at Lillebonne in the Seine-Maritime *département*, where the ruins of a building exist through which runs the main road at the same height as the Toupin hill. To judge by appearances one might think that these are the ruins of a theatre since, roughly speaking, they form a semi-circle. But the existence of a *podium*, a necessary protection against wild beasts, and the elliptical shape of the arena prove that they are nothing of the sort. They are in reality those of an amphitheatre which, according to Grenier, is supposed to have been transformed into a theatre by the removal of a part of the *cavea* and the construction of a stage on its diameter; traces of this stage, which no longer exists, can allegedly be seen on the west side of the building.

Grand, a little village in the Vosges, also possesses a building of this nature, whose general appearance at least is fairly well preserved. It rests against the southern slope of the hill. As the arena has not been excavated, we cannot be sure whether it was bounded by a stage at the point at which the tiers now stop. The monument has an external diameter of 150 yards. That there should be so huge a structure of this kind in this deserted country-side is apt to astonish; the fact is that Grand was at one time a staging-post and a place of pilgrimage where several peoples of eastern Gaul foregathered. It was probably a large town.

But the existence of an important centre was not the condition *sine qua non* of the presence of an amphitheatre. We often find them near the small market-towns which were traditional places of worship among the Gauls, country sanctuaries where they came together, as at Alléan in Touraine or Sanxay in Poitou. The importance of these places of worship in the life of Gaul explains why these two villages had their own theatre-amphitheatre and why Grand should have possessed one of a size almost equal to that of the Arènes de Lutèce in Paris, which fall into the same class of structure. The stage was in the middle of the western tiers. It measured 44 yards—four times more than at Senlis. Staircases linked it with the passage which ran behind the *podium*, where have been found fragments of the capitals and statues that adorned it.

Astonishingly enough, this type of composite building is not found in southern France, which was the most Romanized area; it is mostly to be found in the centre and the north, especially Normandy. The originality of the design is perhaps not due only to a desire for economy; it may also be the fruit of local traditions. That at least is what Grenier thinks: 'For their spectacles the provinces, which had more or less escaped the influence of Rome, had fashioned a type of structure which by combining the classical models completely deformed and transformed them. These theatre-amphitheatres may be considered as an original creation of Gallo-Roman architecture.'

The amphitheatre, instrument of Romanization

Some of these amphitheatres owed their existence to the presence of a garrison. The soldiers themselves put up, for their own entertainment, a rough building, usually wood-framed and of a small size. Sometimes this primitive construction gave birth to a real amphitheatre, as was the case with that of Cimiez, near Nice, the history of which has been reconstructed, thanks to the labours of Paul-Marie Duval; it is a whole made up of two distinct parts, added one to the other and dating from different periods.

But in the eyes of the Romans, the setting up of amphitheatres

o

had above all the advantage of providing an efficient means of reducing local particularism, the power of which Gaul had enabled them to assess. If Autun, for example, which under Augustus became after Bibracte the capital of the Aedui, had the largest amphitheatre in Gaul, it owed this perhaps as much to the desire to encourage a people which had always collaborated with Rome as to its opulence. The historical purpose of the provincial monuments, such as it has recently been defined, could not but have been also that of the amphitheatres, places where people gathered to see the shows and exchange opinions.

'Let us picture the Aeduan peasants coming to the city on market days or days of pilgrimage. . . . How, among these momuments which flattered their vanity, could they have retained the boorish manners of Gallic peasants? Despite themselves, they were won over to the cause of Rome, at first outwardly by a show of manners and then in the depths of their hearts. Among the Romans architecture was an exceptionally effective means of psychological persuasion.'

SHORT GLOSSARY

This glossary is not intended to be exhaustive. It is intended to provide the reader interested in the subject with some of the technical details which the particular treatment of the subject necessarily excluded, especially those relating to the terminology of the 'games'.

Andabate Type of gladiator. See Chapter II.

Balteus Both a gladiator's belt and the wall which divided horizontally the different classes of seats in the amphitheatre.

Bestiarius Man whose profession it was to fight with wild beasts; also a criminal condemned to the beasts.

Biga Two-horse chariot.

Catasta A sort of dais or platform linked to the ground by a ramp, upon which the *retiarius* sometimes fought.

Cavea The tiers of the amphitheatre as a whole, and thus, by extension, the public.

Cochlea A contrivance rather like a revolving door used to confuse the animals.

Confector An attendant of the arena whose task it was to kill the wounded animals.

Consus A god whose altar was in the circus. Perhaps an agrarian deity, perhaps a deity of the under world; according to some, both at the same time.

Dimachaerus A category of gladiators or, according to some, a special fighting technique used by several categories of gladiators.

Doctor Trainer entrusted with perfecting the technique of gladiators and charioteers. When training gladiators the *doctor* specialized in the use of specific weapons.

Editor The *editor* financed, organized and presided over the games. He could be the emperor, a magistrate or a private individual. A special box was reserved for him, facing the emperor's, on the minor axis of the amphitheatre, and it was he who presided over the inspection of the weapons.

Essedarius Type of gladiator. See Chapter II.

Euripus   Trench dug around the outer edge of the race-track of the circus to protect the spectators when 'hunts' were given in the building.

Funalis   Left-hand team horse upon which to a great extent the result of the race depended.

Galerus   A piece of metal, very variable in shape, which protected the left shoulder of a *retiarius* or a *laquearius*; it sometimes covered the neck and protected the wearer from lateral blows.

Games   Free official spectacles, accompanied by religious ceremonies and sometimes by the distribution of public largesse (banquets, *sparsiones*). They were, originally, a religious celebration. Annual, secular or votive, they took, in the course of Roman history, very varied forms.

Games, annual   These were celebrated each year in honour of one god or another, on a date fixed in advance and according to prescribed forms which had, in principle, to be respected. The most important games were: those consecrated to Apollo (*Ludi Apollinares*), to Ceres (*Ludi Cereales* or *Cerealia*), to Flora (*Ludi Florales* or *Floralia*), to Cybele (*Ludi Megalenses* or *Megalesia*); and, finally, the Roman Games (*Ludi Romani* or *Ludi Magni*) and the Games of the Plebeians (*Ludi Plebeii*).

Games, Apollinarian (*Ludi Apollinares*)   Celebrated for the first time in 211 B.C. to ask the Greek Apollo for victory over Hannibal, they were made an annual event in 208 B.C. to ward off a pestilence. They took place from 6 to 13 July and included theatrical presentations, a *venatio* and chariot races.

Games of Ceres (*Ludi Cereales* or *Cerealia*)   Inaugurated to put an end to a period of drought, the *Cerealia*, which took place from 12 to 19 April, were one of the manifestations of the 'agrarian obsession' of which Jean Bayet writes. Before the start of the chariot races which marked the rejoicings foxes with burning torches tied to them were loosed into the arena. According to some, this was a fertility rite.

Games of Flora (*Ludi Florales* or *Floralia*)   Established in honour of the goddess Flora on the occasion of a famine, these festivals, which were celebrated from 28 April to 3 May, included, like the *Cerealia*, many ancient customs; hares and goats, animals with an erotic significance, were hunted in the arena and seed was scattered on the earth as an offering. An atmosphere of primitive licence and pastoral orgy permeated the whole festival; women were clothed in brightly coloured dresses and men were crowned with garlands of flowers; there was hard drinking and, in the theatre, the 'actresses' stripped at the demand of the spectators.

Games, Megalensian
(*Ludi Megalenses*)
These were celebrated from 4 to 10 April in honour of Cybele, whose cult had been introduced into Rome under the pressure of the religious and political distress created by the victories of Hannibal.

Games, Plebeian
(*Ludi Plebeii*)
They were celebrated in November. According to some, they were created by the plebeians after they had been deprived of a wine festival which they celebrated in September and which may have given birth to the *Ludi Romani.*

Games, Roman
(*Ludi Romani* or
Ludi Magni)
Celebrated in September, they sometimes lasted as long as sixteen days. Some people think they originated in a wine festival which the plebeians celebrated in September in honour of the god Liber. Others think that, created in honour of Jupiter Optimus Maximus, they at first had an exceptional and votive character and did not become permanent, according to Livy, until 366 B.C., the date on which the *aediles curules*, who were entrusted with their organization, were created.

Games, Secular
(*Ludi Saeculares*)
Celebrated at the end of a hundred-year cycle, their object was 'to assure the renewal of the world for another cycle'. They were celebrated at night on the Campus Martius round an underground altar called Tarentum or Terentum, which always remained closed except for this event. They were originally offered to the deities of the underworld, Dis Pater and Proserpina, but later the religious policy of the emperors changed their significance and even the intervals at which they occurred.

Games, Votive
(*Ludi Votivi*)
Associated with the history of the first centuries of the Republic, these games had a character all their own: when a peril threatened the Roman state or the result of a war seemed uncertain, the leading magistrates, consuls or dictators, could make a vow to Jupiter or some god of lesser importance to celebrate

213

great games in order to assure his good will. Dependent upon the fulfilment of a wish the God was asked to grant, they were usually celebrated after a delay of five or ten years. The delicate mechanism of this institution was the cause of many conflicts between the magistrates and the Senate.

Hoplomachus Type of gladiator. See Chapter II.

Lanista Proprietor of a troupe of gladiators, not to be confused with the *doctor*, or trainer, of which a certain number formed part of every troupe. It was quite exceptional for a *lanista* himself to organize a spectacle against payment; he rented or sold his troupe to the *editor* under conditions which, in the time of Marcus Aurelius, were subject to fairly strict rules.

Laquearius A type of gladiator whose offensive weapon was a form of lassoo.

Libellus A programme giving the names of the gladiators who
numerarius were to appear in the arena.

Liberatio or Act by which a gladiator was freed from the obliga-
Manumissio tion of fighting in the arena.

Ludi Both the barracks of the gladiators and the *venatores* (imperial *ludi*) and the 'games' themselves (q.v.).

Manica A piece of leather, covered with metal scales, protecting the arm and part of the right hand of the gladiators, which were particularly exposed by the handling of a sword.

Mappa A white cloth which the president of the games threw on to the race-track to give the signal for the races to begin.

Missio The decision by which, in a gladiatorial combat, the public spared the vanquished man. In the combats *sine missione* this reprieve was never given; one of the two adversaries had to remain on the field. In the hunts, *missio* meant the dispatch of a group of animals into the arena.

Missus Start of a chariot race, and, by extension, each of the races making up the spectacle.

Myrmillo, or Type of gladiator. See Chapter II.
Mirmillo

Murrus Combat of gladiators.

Naufragium 'Shipwreck'—circus slang. See Chapter V.

Ocrea A piece of leather reinforced with metal which certain gladiators wore on the left leg, sometimes on both legs. With the Thracians this greave also covered the knee and a part of the thigh.

Palus Training stake for gladiators; it probably also designated the groups into which they were divided.

Pollice verso Expression indicating the gesture of turning the thumb downward by which mercy for a defeated gladiator was refused.

Pompa Ceremonial parade which preceded the spectacles of the circus and the amphitheatre. The circus *pompa* is described in Chapter v. That of the gladiatorial combats, which was accompanied by music, was similar to a military parade but it is difficult to determine its stages and, in particular, to specify at what moment the gladiators pronounced the famous greeting: *Ave Caesar, morituri te salutant.*

Probatio armorum Inspection of weapons by the president of the games.

Provocator Type of gladiator. See Chapter ii.

Retiarius Type of gladiator. See Chapter ii.

Rudis Wooden sword used in training; it was presented as a symbol to a gladiator freed from service in the arena.

Sagittarius A gladiator who fought with a bow.

Samnite (*Samnis*) Type of gladiator. See Chapter ii. Gladiators who were armed with a sword (*gladius*) and a rectangular shield (*scutum*) were said to be 'armed in the Samnite manner'.

Scissor A type of gladiator; not an attendant of the arena.

Secutor Type of gladiator. See Chapter ii.

Silvae Spectacles in the course of which animals were either displayed or hunted in an artificially created pastoral setting.

Sparsio Public largesse in the course of which counters were thrown to the tiers. These counters represented 'lots' of unequal value, varying from a brace of birds to a country house. The custom gave rise to violent quarrels.

Spina The central ridge of the circus. See Chapter v.

Spoliarium The hall near the 'mortuary door' at one of the extremities of the major axis of the amphitheatre where the bodies of gladiators slain in combat were taken. There they were stripped of their arms and those in whom their adversary's sword had left a flicker of life were finished off. This hall was situated exactly opposite the door through which the gladiators entered with great pomp during the parade which preceded the combats.

Suppositicius or *tertiarius* A fresh gladiator whom the victor of a first combat was compelled to face at once.

Thracian (*Thrax*) Type of gladiator. See Chapter II.

Veles Type of gladiator armed with a javelin.

Velum or *velarium* Bands of linen fixed to masts. When they were joined together, they protected the spectators from the sun. Sailors of the fleet manipulated the *velum* as the sun changed position.

Venabulum A stake reinforced by an iron point, used to fight beasts.

INDEX

Italic figures refer to illustration numbers.

KING ALFRED'S COLLEGE
LIBRARY